The Best of www.MyPrayers.net

by Paul Martin

Inspirational Songs, Poems & Prayers
for comfort, joy and peace of mind.

Publisher - www.MyPrayers.net, Paul Martin.

Book design adapted from website, www.MyPrayers.net, by CarolMasonDesign.com.

Contact: Please use the online form on www.MyPrayers.net shown on the "Contact Us" page.

Artwork is licensed or ackowledged on individual pages.

The contents of this book, and more options, are also available on www.MyPrayers.net:
- Print, Download, and Share each Poem & Prayer.
- Listen to each Song in its entirety via Apple Music, Spotify and Youtube.
- Download Complimentary Sheet Music.

This Print Edition Book is available at Local Book Stores.
ISBN 978-0-9979694-1-2
Hard Cover Print Edition

The Digital Edition is available at Online Book Stores.
ISBN 978-0-9979694-9-8

Printed in the United States of America

ACKNOWLEDGEMENTS

This Print Edition Book is adapted from the website www.MyPrayers.net. Almost every piece is written with the intention of helping us to experience God as Love, as we feel His presence in our hearts.

Paul Martin writes Inspirational Poems, Prayers, Essays and Songs exclusively for www.MyPrayers.net.

He produces music and arrangements in collaboration with Daryl Kojak. He collaborates with Carol Mason who designs and maintains www.MyPrayers.net and this book.

Contents

Christ's Life Depicted in Art

Songs

Ten Most Famous Paintings

Essays

Videos

Preface

Dear Reader,

This book is adapted from the content on www.MyPrayers.net which is a website overflowing with spiritual insights, inspirational poems, songs and prayers which engender comfort and peace of mind.

www.MyPrayers.net is somewhat special. It is like a public library or a public park. It is a temple for the craving mind. It is a place we can all return to, again and again, to find relief from the drama of the world and be lifted above the everyday beliefs that disturb our peace of mind.

Unlimited access to every poem, prayer or song and all sheet music is entirely free of charge. We appreciate those who decide to purchase our songs but it is optional and totally a matter of choice. You can hear each entire inspirational song free of charge and without limitation while on our website. It is also a very convenient way to listen. If you access our songs through your various devices it allows you to follow along with the lyrics simultaneously if you so desire.

The Song download features such as iTunes, CDBaby, and Amazon are for the convenience of those who prefer that particular mode of listening. The price of downloading songs is preset by the vendors. If it were our choice there would be no charge. Our printable sheet music will remain free of charge and is quite a popular and rapidly expanding feature. Feel free to add our available songs to your repertoire.

The Print and Share feature is available for the content of each Song, Poem & Prayer and Essay on www.MyPrayers.net.

We've worked hard over the years to keep our www.MyPrayers.net lean and focused. We are fulfilling our mission efficiently thanks to your interest and support.

Now that *The Best of www.MyPrayers* is in a book format you have easy access in a new way. We hope it brings you comfort, joy and peace of mind.

Many Blessings,

www.MyPrayers.net

Painters of religious art shown in this book.

Garofalo Benvenuto Tisi - about (1481 – 1559)
A leading painter working in Ferrara in the earlier 16th century.

Rembrandt Harmenszoon van Rijn (1606 – 1669)
A Dutch draughtsman, painter, and printmaker. He is generally considered one of the greatest visual artists in the history of art and the most important in Dutch art history.

Bartolomé Esteban **Murillo** (1618 – 1682)
A Spanish Baroque painter. Although he is best known for his religious works, Murillo also produced a considerable number of paintings of contemporary women and children.

Johann Michael Ferdinand **Heinrich Hofmann** (1824 – 1911)
A German painter of the late 19th to early 20th century. He is best known for his many paintings depicting the life of Jesus Christ.

Carl Heinrich **Bloch** (1834 – 1890)
A Danish painter. He was then commissioned to produce 23 paintings for the King's Chapel at Frederiksborg Palace. These were all scenes from the life of Christ which have become very popular as illustrations.

V. V. Sapar (19xx – present day)
A fine artist from India-Maharashtra. He speaks through colours, and tell stories through his canvas.

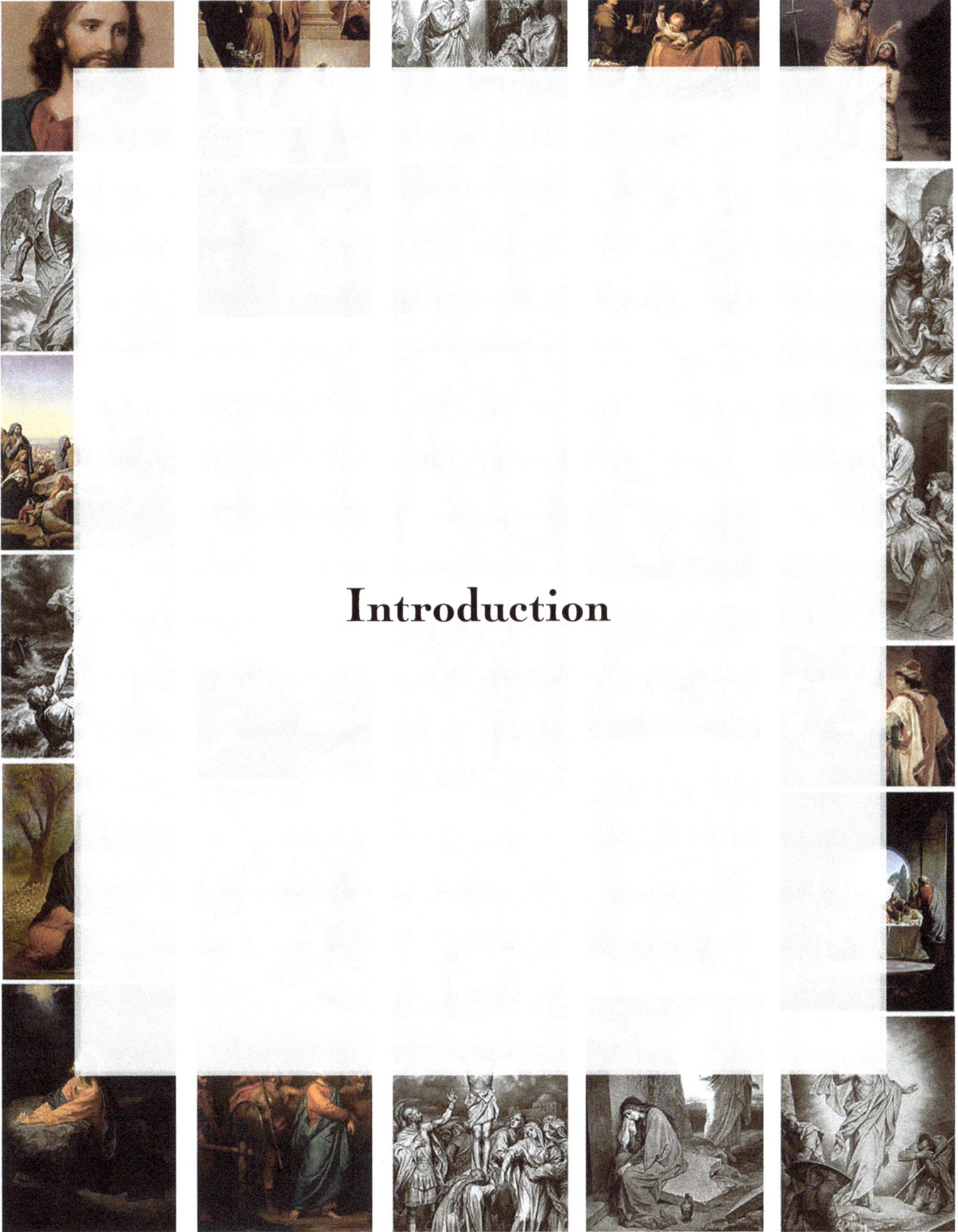

Introduction

Cause-and-Effect

Jesus shone the light of understanding on The Great Law of cause-and-effect and its manifestation when He said "whosoever should have no doubt in his heart but believe what he say cometh to pass, he shall have it."

Whatever it is you're trying to manifest through the use of The Great Law of cause-and-effect, do not be discouraged if you do not get immediate results. Look at it as if you are tipping the scales of trust in your favor, one thought at a time, as the good thoughts outweigh the negative thoughts. The positive balance can be ever so slight in order to bring about a subtle manifestation of the Great Law of cause-and-effect, which manifestation will continue to bear fruit to the degree it is nourished.

Ascension of Christ 1520.
Painting by Garofalo.

Together in Heaven

My dearest friends and family there are things I'd like to say;
first of all I'll let you know I arrived here safe today.
I am sending word from heaven where I'll dwell with God above;
there are no tears and sorrow, there is only peace and love.

I had to leave you as my time on earth was through;
loved ones waited for me just as I will wait for you.
I missed them and I am happy to be with them again;
I want you all to know I'm here with family and friends.

God gave me many tasks he wishes me to do;
high up on the list is watching over all of you.
Don't think I do not hear you because I am out of sight;
remember I am with you every morning, noon and night.

When your load gets heavy don't cry too many tears;
then I can whisper to you what you will need to hear.
I always will be near you to guide you through each day;
remember when you need me I am just a thought away.

Our love will build a highway and our mem
ories a lane;
I'll walk right down from heaven and be with you again.
Remember when you miss me and I am on your mind;
although you will not see me I'll be just a step behind.

When your life on earth is over and your soul is finally free;
believe me when I tell you, you'll be coming home with me.

Also refer to - "The Mortal Dream" by Paul Martin.
Also refer to - "Fallen Angel" by Paul Martin.

Music Credits

The music for "Together in Heaven" was adapted from Beethoven's No. 8 Pathetique by Paul Martin and was produced and arranged by Paul Martin and Daryl Kojak. Daryl's creativity and musicianship are gratefully acknowledged in helping to make possible this epic musical tale of an ascended Soul who is giving comfort to friends and family who were left behind to grieve.

The Ascension 1636.
Painting by Rembrandt.

Inspirational
Poems & Prayers

for comfort, joy and peace of mind.

A Father's Way

As I look back upon my life,
I think of things my father'd say.
He always gave me good advice,
it was just a father's way.

I learned I must have patience-
for good comes to those who wait.
I must be courteous and dependable
and never inconsiderately late.

He'd tell me I must have a heart,
if I'm to demonstrate fair play.
He instilled in me what he was taught,
it was just a father's way.

He'd say my word must be my bond,
for love is based on trust.
To earn the loyalty of others,
one must never be unjust.

He'll live on through his wisdom
and I'm reminded every day,
it was he who gave me character,
it was just a father's way.

Also refer to - "A Mother's Way" by Paul Martin.

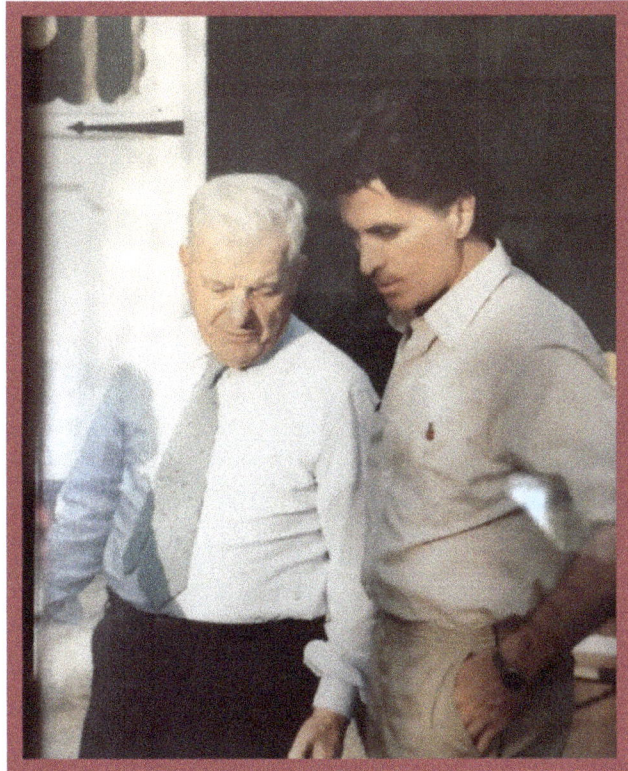

A Mother's Way

Looking back when I was two,
there is one thing I surely knew,
I craved the love of my mother,
which was comforting and true.

She'd nurture me with kindness
and with words not understood.
I longed to speak her language
and felt sure someday I would.

She calmed me and cured me,
in part by what she'd say,
she made me feel I was loved,
it was just A Mother's Way.

What was it she was saying
that made me feel so good?
Could it be her heartfelt love,
that I intuitively understood?

The years have flown by quickly,
yet it seems like yesterday;
when Mother would comfort me,
this is often what she'd say,

"Love will enlighten you,
when you sincerely pray.
God will always care for you,
it is just A Mother's Way."

Also refer to - "A Father's Way" by Paul Martin.

IMAGE № 3 - Christ's Life Depicted in Art

The Visit of the Three Wise Men.
Drawing by Heinrich Hofmann.

Angels

She was an angel all in white,

possessing warmth and dignity.

She was the epitome of purity,

reflecting innocence and glee.

She was curious and comforting,

as she whispered softly to me.

She shared inspired thoughts,

I felt as though she knew me.

Why did she appear to me?

I would really like to know.

My one regret was when she left,

I did not want to see her to go.

Beckoning Tree

Beckoning tree whispering its

welcome with yearning rustling

to the itinerant birds at nightfall,

offering them tranquil shelter.

How gentle is its loving caress.

How its enfolding leaves lull its

weary guests to trustful repose.

How majestic it stands,

accommodating and mindful

of its unwavering expression

of selfless devotion.

Contemplation

Our natural state of being is to bask in the radiant joy of peace, love and harmony. I have within me a higher and a lower nature which are occasionally at odds. My higher nature thrives on Love while my lower nature struggles with fear. As my higher nature becomes increasingly evolved I am able to cultivate blissful love as I rise above delusive fear through peaceful contemplation. When unfettered my soul is omniscient and beholds God through intuition.

In order to feel Love I can choose to focus my thoughts on higher truths. In intuitional communion I align my thoughts, actions, life and will with God's words of spiritually awakening truth until I know with certainty the kingdom of heavenly bliss can be experienced in the precious here and now.

I then perceive all of creation as being precisely and lovingly orchestrated by God and his angels. This obscure Divine Order is reminiscent of an ever changing, yet always luminously flawless, kaleidoscope. I see all creation as reflecting an endless variety of scenes and patterns, a succession of changing phases and actions, shifting values and information, constantly methodically evolving, being eternally uplifting and unfathomably precise.

I get a glimpse of the perfection we are all interconnected with and I am reminded eternal life is a great adventure which becomes progressively more rewarding as we climb the unimaginable heights of spiritual evolution. This perceivable perfection has led me to the inescapable conclusion that each moment of life is meant to be cherished, for it is all good. No matter what difficulty we are faced with at the moment there will always be a light at the end of the tunnel. Divine Order is correcting and adjusting for the purpose of restoring the lost clarity of divine sight which is ours to reclaim.

As we progress in spiritual insights and wisdom life gets better and our trials become less burdensome. We become more deeply immersed in Love and light until eventually we are free to live with God in a paradise of contemplation. One has only to lift the opaque veil of delusion and uncertainty to bask in the glowing and blissful bright, fountain of light, love, hope, peace and joy. We are blessed by the harmonious balance of infinite wisdom and love of our indwelling Divinity as we progressively revel in the heavenly freedom of infinity.

Also refer to - "Illumination" by Paul Martin.

Photos by Paul Martin

Cosmic Consciousness

There is a state of consciousness, so joyful, so glorious, that all lesser expressions of awareness are worthless in comparison. It is "a pearl of great price," which the wise man willingly gives up all he has to acquire. The enlightened prophets who walked the earth at various times throughout the history of mankind had one common purpose. It was to impart to us, through divine revelation and compassionate demonstration, a realization of the uncompromising void that permeates our lives as a result of our not possessing this glorious state of awareness, which can be more specifically understood to be the pure Cosmic Consciousness of the Kingdom of God.

When the whole of humanity eventually acquires Cosmic Consciousness all religions and traditions will simply fade away and will be replaced by a mutually possessed super-consciousness that will neither be believed nor disbelieved, but rather experienced. It will not be a part of life belonging to a particular few hours of the week, nor will it reside in sacred books entrusted to a few appointed holy men and women. It will not depend on prayers, books, preachers or prophets, nor will there be a mission to save men from their sins or secure entrance into heaven for them. The realization of immortality will be alive in every heart and having the least bit of doubt with regard to eternal life will be as impossible as being doubtful of momentary existence.

Cosmic Consciousness will permeate each moment of everyone's life and intermediaries between God and man will be permanently replaced by directly flowing, enlightening, nurturing and loving intercourse between man and his Creator. Humanity will possess an unwavering consciousness of their ever-evolving immortality. There will be absolutely no concern about what comes after this mortal sojourn being as all will be privileged to see beyond the veil in dreams and visions.Ascension to a higher realm of eternal life will be optimistically welcomed as a path to greater freedom, happiness and spiritual expansion. It will occur at an appropriate time which one will be aware of and voluntarily submit to with great anticipation and joyful expectations.

The inevitable transition of humanity to the possession of Cosmic Consciousness began with a few God-realized individuals. They were the prophets of old who have since inspired many to rise above the human condition. As a result the number of enlightened souls possessing Cosmic Consciousness is growing exponentially as more and more evolve spiritually to the point where they possess this exalted state of enlightenment. Through uncompromising dedication and willingness to trust the enlightened ones who came before us we are able to attain entrance into the ever-beckoning liberation, joy, shelter and guidance of the pure Cosmic Consciousness of the Kingdom of God.

We will have unleashed the true nature of our soul, the "image of God" within, and in doing so have banished the insidiously destructive forces that heretofore have threatened our well-being. We will have resurrected the empowering benevolent forces of divine love, wisdom, peace and the inestimable joy of nurturing communion with the Cosmic Consciousness of our Creator. We will have discovered the elusive and heretofore seemingly indefinable purpose of life.

Note: Christ Consciousness is synonymous with Cosmic Consciousness and is referred to as Enlightenment in Eastern philosophy.

IMAGE № 11 - Christ's Life Depicted in Art

The Sermon on the Mount.
Painting by Carl Bloch.

Faith and Trust

I have faith in your power,
I trust I'll be restored.
Let your love enjoin me,
keep me close forevermore.

Let me awaken to thy blessings,
reveal my true identity.
Let me glow with Holy Spirit,
as I perceive eternity.

Let me bind myself to thee,
as I utilize your power.
Let your love embrace me,
like the fragrance in a flower.

Let Life and Light shine through me,
reflecting perfect harmony.
Through communion and surrender,
I will find my way to thee.

I have faith in your power,
I trust in your eternal care,
as light destroys the darkness
and limitations disappear.

The power of God and ambition,
do not go hand in hand.
Let me be a humble servant,
for the benefit of man.

IMAGE № 27 - Christ's Life Depicted in Art

The Arrest of Jesus.
Painting by Heinrich Hofmann.
Courtesy of Hessisches Landesmuseum Darmstadt.

Fallen Angel

I am a fallen Angel,
I've reaped what I have sown.
I left my home in paradise,
for the lure of the unknown,

I was enticed by sensuality,
it seemed like a better life.
If only I had known about
the toils, snares and strife.

It seems I wasn't satisfied
to be blissful and inspired.
I should have known this world
would leave a lot to be desired.

Who can better understand
the life for which I yearn?
Than all the fallen Angels
who are longing to return.

Someday, I will find my way
back to The Promised Land
Now that I have been here,
I will not come back again.

I am a fallen Angel,
I seek assurance from above.
I long to be with God again,
to be enveloped by His Love.

Familiarity Breeds Contempt

This saying has its origins in one of Aesop's fables:

"When first the Fox saw the Lion he was terribly frightened, and ran away and hid himself in the wood. Next time however he came near the King of Beasts he stopped at a safe distance and watched him pass by. The third time they came near one another the Fox went straight up to the Lion and passed the time of day with him, asking him how his family was, and when he should have the pleasure of seeing him again; then turning his tail, he parted from the Lion without much ceremony."

More than likely the deeper spiritual meaning is as follows:

I cannot make you happy, I can only make you happier. Through the ages God-centered people have had one thing in common, they do not depend on others for their happiness. Their first love is their spiritual communion with God, its resultant joy, wisdom and inevitable contribution to humanity.

Therefore, I will take responsibility for my inner life. I will not make you my God. This burden is too much for you to bear and is more than I should expect from you. If I depend on you for my happiness, I will resent you when I am feeling unhappy. If we hold each other responsible for our unhappiness, our bond will wither and die.

If I depend on divine union for happiness, I will not expect you to make me happy. I will always be grateful to you for the times when you have increased my happiness. I will feel no resentment for anyone, especially those who mean the most to me. I will enjoy the mutual support of those like-minded people with whom I share a bond of love, admiration and respect.

Forever Young

The secret of true happiness,
is remembering who you are.
Knowing you are a child of God,
and you are Forever Young.

Whenever you feel all alone,
just sing this little song.
Remember deep down in your soul,
you'll be Forever Young.

No matter what remember,
you are a child of God.
You know life is forever,
and you are Forever Young.

Keep remembering life's forever,
you'll feel peace and joy and Love.
You will find true happiness,
and you'll be Forever Young.

Artist's rendering by Francesco Romoli

Forgive Us Our Trespasses

The God seeking individual, by prayerfully intuitive perception,
explores the depths of his soul and gathers all offensive tendencies
which are methodically consumed by the flames of fiery wisdom.

The innate purity of each of us devoted to truth emerges from behind the
clouds of delusion and shines forth as the eradicating Sun of wisdom.

For those who possess spiritual readiness, let them experience truth
through the direct perception of purifying and enlightening intuition.

So it is, when we realize the error of our ways, we are forgiven.
We are purified by eternally blossoming understanding.

"Joy replaces sorrow, as light replaces darkness,
when understanding is rewarded with forgiveness."*

* Refer to - "The Lord's Prayer - A guide to experiencing the blissful presence of God." by Paul Martin.

IMAGE № 14 - Christ's Life Depicted in Art

Jesus Forgives the Sinful Woman.
Drawing by Heinrich Hofmann.

God Loves Me

I have no doubt God loves me,
He shows me every day.
I am His faithful servant,
He uses me in many ways.

I pray to Him each day and say,
make use of me as you will today.
Devotion is all you require of me,
as you patiently mold my destiny.

You are the potter, I am the clay.
You inspire me in so many ways.
You mold me as I deserve to be,
I too use you, as you use me.

As a cart must follow its drawing horse,
I am the expression of my thoughts.
The path to you is mine to choose,
your power is ever mine to use.

I feel your presence everywhere,
because of you I have no fear.
I call upon you night and day,
keep me safe and guide my way.

IMAGE № 7 - Christ's Life Depicted in Art

The Boy Jesus with the Doctors in the Temple.
Painting by Heinrich Hofmann.

Good Deeds

Cause and Effect, a.k.a., Karma is an uncompromising law whereby the consequences of thoughts and actions sown are reaped precisely in kind.* In order to receive good things back in kind, we need to attract other good people into our lives. The more good we do, the more we attract good into our lives. Our good thoughts and actions ripple through humanity and create a chain reaction. We are creators made in the image and likeness of our Creator. We may believe our thoughts and actions are inconsequential, the reality is we can play an important role in uplifting humanity.**

The good deed we did this morning may have been passed on and on and made its way around the entire world by evening. It would follow that everyone who passes a good deed on to others creates their own little chain reaction. Before long our personal world becomes filled with good people who are connected by their good deeds, yet may have no idea of the far-reaching effects their actions are inconspicuously weaving. We are all emissaries of God and with love, we can create a better world.

The interesting part is it doesn't matter if you are aware of the underlying effects, you will still be a very positive force for change. The choices you make determine the effects you cause and therefore determine the quality of your world. The long term effects of your choices will ripple down through humanity for centuries and beyond and actually change the course of many lives, and inadvertently, history itself. The reality is we all can play a truthful and significant part in uplifting the consciousness of humanity and enhancing the resultant unfoldment of history.

It may come as a surprise that the highest expression of a good deed is rooted in being careful not to hurt others by continually putting yourself in their shoes. Ask yourself, "Would I like this done to me?" This is the true test of right and wrong in God's eyes and will always supersede the hypocrisy of conscienceless delusion which is often unwittingly imposed upon us by our forefathers. We reap the consequences of inherited, mindless, inconsiderate and hypocritical thoughts and actions. Herein lies the true meaning of the Biblical pronouncement, "We suffer for the sins of our Fathers." The reality is sin is nothing more than ignorance of God's unalterable laws of Cause and Effect.

Simply put, we must take care not to hurt others if we want to have an increasingly meaningful life. Eventually, we all will understand, "the love we receive is precisely equal to the love we give."***

* Refer to - "Truth or Consequences" by Paul Martin.
** Refer to - "The Mortal Dream" by Paul Martin.
*** Refer to - "God's Love" by Paul Martin.

IMAGE № 10 - Christ's Life Depicted in Art

Healing the Sick.
Drawing by Heinrich Hofmann.

Heroes

God watches over his children,
and every now and then,
He knows things will be better,
If he lends a helping hand.

From among us comes a Hero,
and in time we understand,
we should follow in his footsteps,
for he is no ordinary man.

His light may shine just briefly,
yet he's never really gone.
For those of us who love him,
his memory will live on.

At first we may not realize,
yet as time goes on we see,
his exemplary life inspires us,
to be all that we can be.

He may have suffered greatly
to implement God's plan.
Yet then, we must remember,
he was no ordinary man.

Our Hero never compromised,
never wandered from his path.
In our hearts we understand,
he was no ordinary man.

Abraham Lincoln.

The Lincoln Memorial building is an American memorial built to honor the 16th President of the United States, Abraham Lincoln. It is located on the National Mall in Washington, D.C. and was dedicated on May 30, 1922. The architect was Henry Bacon, the sculptor of the main statue (Abraham Lincoln, 1920) was Daniel Chester French, and the painter of the interior murals was Jules Guerin. The building is in the form of a Greek Doric temple and contains a large seated sculpture of Abraham Lincoln and inscriptions of two well-known speeches by Lincoln, The Gettysburg Address and his Second Inaugural Address.

I am a Soul

I am a soul, I was never born,
therefore, I can never perish.
I am an immortal individual,
bound to all I love and cherish.

I've played many roles,
in many times and lands.
When this journey's over,
I'll be going home again.

I've traveled to the shores,
of storm tossed humanity.
I left my home in paradise,
along with all my memories.

I've progressed with dedication,
I see through my mortal guise.
I express increased divinity,
as I strive to help mankind.

Now I need not worry,
about what's beyond the veil.
I realize I am imperishable,
I'm an immortal, ageless soul.

Mark Twain as a young man.

Mark Twain was the first American writer to infuse in his characters wit, humor, wisdom, heart and Soul and feelings, regardless of their color. In all probability, his creativity and insight into human nature remain unparalleled to this day. Haley's Comet flashed across the sky at the hour of his birth and likewise, at the hour of his passing some seventy years later. I can't help but wonder if his Soul arrived and departed via some sort of divinely orchestrated special delivery.

I Have A Dream

To my grandson, Ryan,

I truly believe our country desperately needs a message of appreciation for the freedom which we so often take for granted. I dream of our country being healed and our people being united as Americans, one nation, under God, as it was always intended to be. I hope and pray, one day, a united USA can make the world safe for your generation.

Maybe you can help to make my dream come true. Do you have a dream? Maybe I can help you with your dream when you eventually get one that has a deep meaning to you. Try and make it one that will help other people, then God will surely be on your side.

"I am proud to be an American,

I know a house divided cannot stand.

Can we walk together hand-in-hand,

in the Freedom of the USA?"*

* Refer to - "The Freedom of the USA" by Paul Martin.

Illumination

If a child were to ask me how a certain food tastes, could I adequately describe it? Or, must it be an individual experience? With this in mind, should I emulate the great Seers, such as but not limited to, Jesus, Buddha and Krishna? Was their sole purpose to shed light on how we may bring the living presence of God into our thoughts and actions, as exemplified by their lives? Were they a connecting link between God and man? Were they Divine enough to know God and human enough to impart their knowing to man? Should I follow worldly people whose focus is on the perishable things of life? Can the spiritually blind lead the spiritually blind? Or, should I trust in those enlightened ones whose focus was on the imperishable? Should I fervently seek to embrace the spiritual path of the imperishable aspects of the source of lifeband light within me? Will this path eventually lead me to experience illumination for myself? Is illumination a matter of experiencing and expressing the blissful, healing and guiding light within in order to unite ourselves with Divinity?

Am I similar to a light bulb without which electricity cannot be seen? Am I therefore, an individual expression of God, who is my source of life and light? Am I connected to all other individual expressions of God by virtue of our commonly shared source of life and light? Are we therefore, of one mind and indwelling spirit? When God's light is no longer able to shine through my eventually to be abandoned bodily abode, is it conceivable He and/or I will cease to exist? Or, will the immortal consciousness of my Soul assume a finer form of visible expression and return to Him within the bliss of the paradisiacal Promised Land?

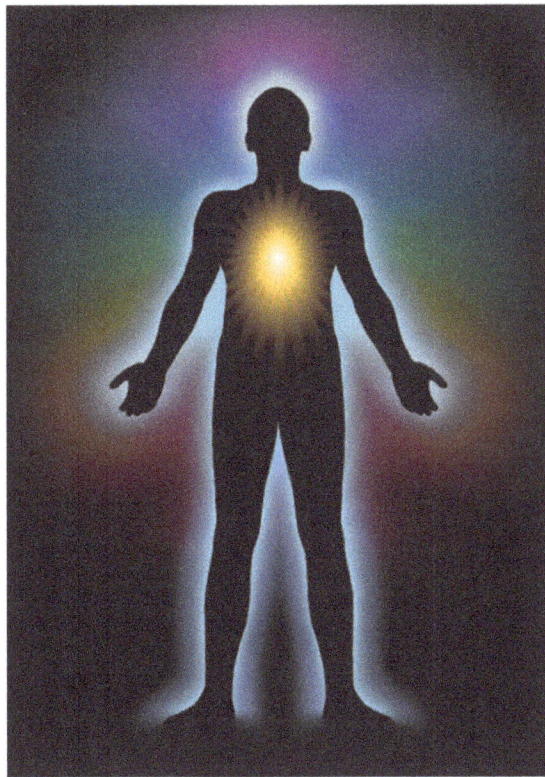

Imagine Mother Mary's Life

She was very young and according to God's plan,
was soon to be betrothed to a gentle, older man.
While in the midst of angels, she truly understood,
she would be sanctified by her virgin motherhood.

Away in a manger she gave birth to a prophet son.
How could she imagine that she would be the one,
to stand by Jesus faithfully until his work was done?
She was to be a mother who would glorify her son.

She watched as he matured into a miraculous man.
His fame was soon to spread all throughout the land.
What trials and tribulations was she able to foresee?
How could she imagine he would love his enemies?

It's hard to imagine how she suffered from her loss,
As she witnessed her beloved Jesus die upon the cross.
Our lives were changed forever by her redeeming son,
was his work on earth completed, or had it just begun?

On the second night, she awoke with the first light,
It appeared he had risen, she believed he was alive.
I can imagine her relief, for as Jesus prophesied,
he fulfilled his promise to demonstrate eternal life.

Within the lonely, longing hours of her later years,
I imagine our ascended savior would often reappear.
He would sit and talk with his beloved matriarch,
I am sure he'd assure her, she is always in his heart.

This poem was inspired by insights within a lyric
called "I can't Imagine" by Dr. Michael McDonough.

IMAGE № 3 - Christ's Life Depicted in Art

The Visit of the Three Wise Men.
Drawing by Heinrich Hofmann.

Immortality

Do you know with certainty you are an immortal being? Are you devoted to nourishing a deepening awareness of this eternal truth? It is helpful to understand the allegorical nature of the story of Adam and Eve.

God created Adam and Eve in his own image and likeness (as immortals). He created the Garden of Eden (paradise) where they could live in eternal harmony. He warned them not to partake of the forbidden fruit of the tree of good and evil (carnal knowledge), or they would soon forget their immortal heritage and become entranced in a dream of mortality (original sin). This pervasive unawareness of their immortality would become the agonizing and heretofore bequeathed delusive plague of mortal man's thinking (fear of death).

Therefore, to transcend this dream of mortality (hell), should be our primary goal in life. Once we awaken from this insidious illusion (belief in death), we are free to live in an ever expanding paradise of contemplation (love) which is ours by divine right.

We will have restored the lost clarity of divine sight (intuitive wisdom), which is always ours to reclaim. We will bask in the blissful glow of eternally enlightening truth (grace). We will trust in God's eternally sheltering love and guidance (consciousness of immortality).

IMAGE № 30 - Christ's Life Depicted in Art

The Resurrection.
Drawing by Heinrich Hofmann.

Is God Our Faithful Servant?

Many believe the events of our lives are predetermined and whatever happens, either good or bad, is God's will. Fortunately, nothing could be further from the truth. Is it possible God is our servant? Does he mold us as we deserve to be? Should we become fitting instruments for God's power to express itself?

God's will for us is the unalterable outcome of the thoughts and actions we lay upon the altar of His great law of cause-and-effect. His will expresses itself through the choices we make and we are always responsible for our actions. We provide the material by which He molds our destiny.

We don't always get what we want but we do get what we create according to the thoughts and actions we have given God to shape our destiny with. His will coincides with ours when we are perfectly in tune with His great law of cause-and-effect.

What we experience is not of His choosing but ours. We must trust in the fact that through Him we can create good, which he will implement on our behalf, for He knows nothing of evil.

Wisdom lies in the careful consideration of the effect of every cause and the willingness to adjust ourselves accordingly. The Great Law is our connection by which we mold our destiny. It's the source of God's protection; as we believe, so we will be.

IMAGE № 20 - Christ's Life Depicted in Art

Christ and the Rich Young Man.
Painting by Heinrich Hofmann.

Joyful Poems

"Thou shalt love the Lord thy God with all thy heart, with all thy soul and all thy mind and have no other Gods before you" is possible to demonstrate when we understand the exact nature of God, what our relationship to Him is and what is the extent of the power He places at our disposal. It is essential that we understand God, so when we dwell on Him in prayerful meditation we will be correcting all the worldly misconceptions we are continually exposed to.

Joyful poems that are of a spiritual nature can help us to understand how to open the aperture that separates us from God, in order to allow His love, bliss and wisdom to flow through us. We learn the true meaning of prayer is not to ask for specific requests but rather to be able bask in blissful and enlightening God contact.

This Communion with God automatically corrects our difficulties in life, some of which we are aware of and some which we are not. When we place more faith in someone or something other than God, we violate the First Commandment, and as a result we are blocked from God's love, protection and empowerment.

Spiritually joyful poems are poems of encouragement, whose underlying meaning ensure us the more we are attuned to God's will, as a result of our right thoughts and actions, the more we experience Him as love, peace and joy. We grow to understand our thoughts and actions are returned to us precisely in kind. All one has to do to rise above the human condition is to turn to God conscientiously and He will reward our noble thoughts and actions. No longer will we need to look for love in all the wrong places. To achieve salvation is to experience the loving and guiding presence of God and to understand the many blessings that are available to us through His unconditional love.

We learn to use the power and the wisdom offered to us by God for everyone's benefit and not only for ourselves. We demonstrate genuine prayers for humanity by our exalted thoughts and actions, which invariably work for the benefit of all mankind. How can we possibly do anything other than to express our love and devotion to God once we truly understand the absolute degree to which we are safe in his eternally sheltering love and guidance?

IMAGE № 23 - Christ's Life Depicted in Art

Jesus' Entry into Jerusalem.
Drawing by Heinrich Hofmann.

Judgment Day

When I was a just a little boy, I was swimming with my friends,
we held hands and formed a circle and round and round we went.
Panic gripped a playmate who could no longer touch the ground,
she clung to me so desperately, as she was dragging me down.

I had swallowed lots of water and much to my surprise,
every moment of my lifetime flashed before my very eyes.
I reviewed every interaction, with everyone I'd ever known,
gentle judgments guided me to see, I'd reaped what I had sown.

Time was standing still, or I never could have seen,
every moment of my life pass by, as if within a dream.
I could see so clearly now the error of my ways,
in my heart I realized, this was the Judgment Day.

There was no hope of survival, yet I did not seem to mind,
I was enraptured and enlightened by what was going through my mind.
Out of nowhere came a lifeguard, after what seemed eternity,
He made a timely rescue and interrupted Judgment Day.

Many years have passed since then, but time has not erased,
the memories of what I saw and learned, on that fateful day.
They've guided me insightfully, in a consequential and enduring way.
I knew I'd never be the same, and I'd remember Judgment Day.

IMAGE № 18 - Christ's Life Depicted in Art

Become as Little Children.
Drawing by Heinrich Hofmann.

Kings and Queens

A good King must possess the wisdom of Solomon.
His judgments are always insightful and impartial.
His uppermost desire is for the welfare of his subjects.

If he must select a Queen he should choose from
among those who possess character and integrity.
He should desire a woman who is fit to be his Queen.
Someone strong enough to allow herself to be feminine,
and wise enough to counsel him in the midst of his trials.

He cherishes his Queen and she respects him as her King.
She gives him the support he needs to shield her from the world
and the insights he requires to use his power wisely.
He protects her so she will not lose her child like innocence,
for within her innocence lies the wisdom of the ages.

There are times when a King may need to walk alone.
If he cannot do this, he is not fit to be a King.
He can live without a Queen if need be,
although this is never his first choice or desire.
He knows a King without a loyal Queen is somewhat like
a storm tossed ship that must struggle to stay its course,
or a faltering sail without a full wind to propel its journey.

Who Ever Loved, That Loved Not at First Sight?

an interpretation

It lies not in our power to love or hate,
Our feelings are subject to forces beyond our control

For will in us is overruled by fate,
Will power is overruled by the inevitability of fate

When two are stripped long ere the course begins,
Mutual desire signals the birth of a joining that binds

We wish that one should lose, the other win;
We wish life to revolve around ourselves

And one especially do we affect
The more one loves us the more we affect them

Like two gold ingots, alike in each respect;
Cast in the same mold we are entranced by our alikeness

The reason no man knows let it suffice
It should be sufficient there is no reasonable explanation

What we behold is censured by our eyes,
We are drawn to some and not to others

Where both deliberate, the love is slight;
The love is slight if we are unsure of how we feel

Who ever loved, that loved not at first sight?
Love at first sight bypasses the thoughts
and goes directly to the heart

From "Hero and Leander" by Christopher Marlowe.

"Dante meets Beatrice at Ponte Santa Trinita."
by Henry Holiday, 1883, oil on canvas,
National Museums and Galleries on Merseyside, Liverpool.

Love Is A Magnetic Force

God is Love,

our source of Life.

Love is a magnetic force,

It draws us closer.

It ultimately awakens us,

it summons us toward

a luminous portal,

to the embracing Light

of Life beyond the veil,

the unfathomable Peace

of individuality abiding

in the tranquility of Love,

in paradise,

forever.

Man's Best Friend

I am your average well-adjusted canine and am otherwise known as a dog.
I come from a good family and have a wonderful disposition.
Now I would like to tell you about the secret life of dogs.

It is a well known fact we give our masters immeasurable unconditional love.
We are faithful and make good companions. We are able to read their minds
and are usually aware of what they are thinking before they know themselves.
We sense when they are on their way home even if they are many miles away.
We have an uncanny ability to find our way home even from faraway places.

We cannot express ourselves verbally but we do express ourselves behaviorally and,
more importantly, we communicate telepathically. One way or another, we manage
to make our feelings known. We are capable of executing many sophisticated tasks,
although we prefer this to be a labor of love reserved exclusively for our masters.
We remain devoted to our masters even at times when they do not return our love.

We are life's unsung heroes as we have done much to consistently comfort humanity.
We are not complicated, we simply enjoy giving love and will do just about anything
we possibly can to receive it. Once we give our love we never withhold it as this can
cause a great deal of unhappiness. We are perfectly willing to have our lives revolve
around the lives of our masters and we remain devoted to them until the very end.

We see all God's children as equal and have no preferences as to race, color or creed.
It is appropriate we are considered to be among life's truly unconditional lovers and
it is no small wonder we are affectionately and deservedly called "Man's Best Friend."

Meditation

Consciousness raising truths to memorize

I am an individual expression of the transcendent and blissful Spirit of God.
He is my creator and the source of the immortal consciousness of my Soul.
My Soul is the master of my mind and my mind is the master of my body.

God is the life force within the unseen power of creation and He expresses
Himself constructively through my intuitively monitored thoughts and actions.
My thoughts are infused with creative power and I affirm this in meditation.

My unwavering trust in God's willingness to enable me to manifest well-being
is the catalyst which opens the floodgates of His empowering life force, that
which gives light and guidance to my mind and life and healing to my body.

A blissful peace, light and healing presence fill me with the joy of knowing
I am not a powerless victim of circumstance, but rather a beloved child of God.
My trust is rewarded with mastery over seemingly insurmountable obstacles.

His power flows through me, I am eternally safe in His loving care and guidance.
The everlasting now, becomes the jubilant existence it was always meant to be.
My rejoicing heart is immersed in the tranquility of His abounding presence.
I am sustained and transformed by the boundlessly loving Grace of God.

Meditation   www.MyPrayers.net

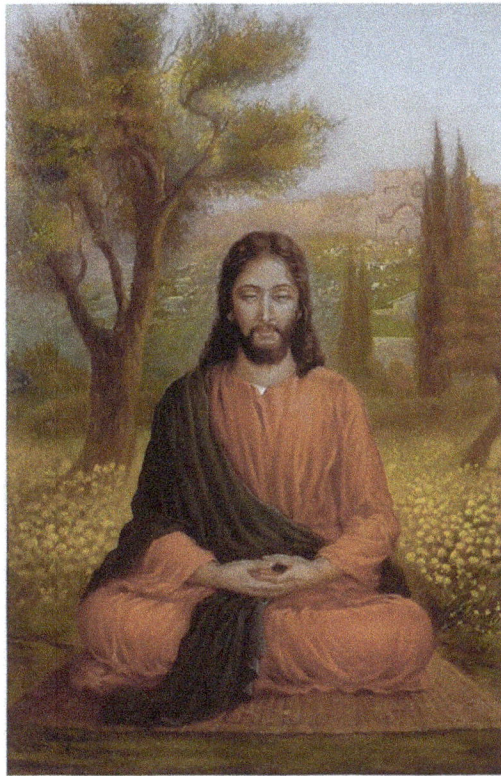

IMAGE № 21 - Christ's Life Depicted in Art

❀

Jesus in the Interiorization of Prayer in Meditation.
Painting by V. V. Sapar.

Meditate "How to"

Genetic restoration

If you had hopes of climbing Mount Everest, would you look for a guide who has actually climbed to the top or would you settle for one who has gone a half or a third of the way, or possibly none of the way? Is it the same with meditation? Can an instructor take you only as far as he or she has gone themselves? Should we follow the example of the prophets of old such as, but not limited to, Jesus, Buddha and Krishna? They left us a very profound legacy, in both word and deed, with regard to their ongoing communion with their heavenly Father. Communion with God and its resultant exchange is a worthy goal as it is the essential element of meditation. It is the result of our concentrating on eternal truths.

The actual meaning of the word "meditate" is to engage in thought or contemplation with deeply focused concentration. Many well-meaning instructors believe in order to meditate, you must clear your mind of all thoughts. It seems likely they have not yet scaled the heavenly heights of consciousness themselves, for it is impossible to think about nothing at all. When you think about nothing, you're actually thinking about something, being as your mind is occupied with attempting to think about nothing.

When meditating upon Truth, we must suspend all negative beliefs until they are swept peacefully away in the wake of our increasingly unwavering trust. The reality is we should always focus our thoughts on the fact that we are heirs to Divine power. As we meditate upon this obscure blessing, we will feel elated and intoxicated with the joy of experiencing and expanding upon this enabling and enhancing empowerment. As God's heirs, we must be devoted to establishing the interchange of communion with Him. We must trust His hand is ever available and always at work and ready to bring peace and rest to our Soul.

On MyPrayers.net, you will find many poems, songs, and prayers which will increase your understanding of God and our relationship to Him. When we dwell on these sacred truths in meditation, we lift the veil of delusion, that which clouds our thoughts with fear and uncertainty. It will be helpful to study one of our works in particular. It is appropriately called "Meditation." If one commits it to memory and meditates upon the truths therein, they will be lifted above the human condition. Eventually, they will view life from an eternal vantage point. All the ancient prophets, those who originally shed light on these truths, will be their guides. The wisdom of the Sages will inspire them in order that they may scale the highest peaks of consciousness, on an ever enlightening basis, as they commune with God in ever intensifying meditation.

We must concentrate deeply and regularly upon the highest truths we can aspire to in order to reap the resultant wisdom, peace, joy, healing and bliss which emanate from and are the much desired outcome of communing with God in meditation. It will also be beneficial to become familiar with our comprehensive interpretation of Jesus' propitious insights entrusted to us in "The Lord's Prayer." As previously mentioned, please enjoy the many other enlightening interpretations of Truth which can be found on MyPrayers.net. The uppermost goal one can aspire to in life is to experience just one tiny

IMAGE № 24 - Christ's Life Depicted in Art

The Last Super: "And He Took The Cup . . ."
Drawing by Heinrich Hofmann.

moment of the blissful and effulgent light of God contact. You will feel an immediate transformation of both mind and body. From that moment on, you will look forward to meditating, for your main desire will be to cultivate and thereby experience wholeness through the equally flowing exchange of communion with God. If one consecrates their life to the service and worship of God, they will be privy to a great power within. When we are able to connect to this omnipresent power, all ills are healed and all burdens are relieved.

✤ ✤ ✤

Your notes

_____

_____

_____

_____

_____

_____

_____

_____

_____

_____

_____

Mona Lisa's Eyes

Leonardo and I loved each other. You can see it in my eyes. We felt much more vibrant when we were in each other's presence. He painted my portrait while viewing me through inspired eyes which were visually enhanced by the intensity of his love for me. He captured the essence of my soul. He created a surreal likeness which was intended to be a vehicle by which I could return from the world beyond to visit him if I were to predecease him. All he need do was to gaze longingly at my image and in that moment I would will myself to be there with him, viewing, feeling, sensing, exchanging the peace and warmth that flows between two longing souls who are capable of such extreme depth of feelings and emotion.

Great artists such as Leonardo have a miraculous ability to command their brushes to conform to the precise demands of their amplified vision. He was able to create an enduring, potentially life imbued, portrait which I continue to revisit on occasion. It takes a great yearning on the part of the viewer to entice me to return to the painting, especially now that Leonardo and I are together in heaven along with others we have known and loved. However, I am concernedly available to warm the hearts of those who are truly in need of love and inspiration. If you concentrate on me and reveal the intensity of your desire, I will return. I will maintain eye contact with you and follow you across the room if need be. I will comfort you with my smiling eyes as I mirror and amplify your emotions. You will feel loved.

The inspired ability to enable a soulfully emotional presence to shine forth visibly from its likeness was by no means possessed exclusively by Leonardo. In the day and age we lived in, the premature death of our loved ones was a constant and burdensome concern. Sanitary conditions were poor and famine, war and pestilence were rampant. As a result, our lives were randomly and prematurely cut short. No one was exempt from this brutally ongoing game of chance, regardless of social standing or wealth. Those who could afford the services of a great artist would commission paintings of their loved ones in the event they were prematurely taken. They would then be able to commune with them at will in order to provide some small degree of comfort and to lessen their sorrow in their time of loss. Quite often paintings were life size and displayed in the most elegant surroundings.

We cherished those we loved as we fervently expressed our interminable devotion. We were grateful for every moment we shared being as we were constantly reminded of the fragility of mortal life. As a result of our trials we possessed an unwavering realization of the reality of eternal life and an intuitive understanding a portrait by an inspired artist was a bridge between heaven and earth. It was an instrument which would serve to nourish our bonds of love until such time as those of us who were left behind would be reunited with those who had gone on ahead to prepare the way.

Mona Lisa.
Painting by Leonardo da Vinci.

My Life As A Car

I am a car.

I have no personality of my own.
I am forced to express the moods of my drivers.
I provide protection for them and as a result
I am also forced to take unnecessary risks.
They sometimes do awful things they ordinarily
would not do without me there to protect them.
They break laws right and left, no pun intended.

They usually sneak through caution lights,
and sometimes even red lights and stop signs.
I have to hold my breath as most of the time it is
I who gets hurt and occasionally it is both of us.

Courtesy seems to be totally forgotten, for
a gentlemen who will open a lady's door
will run the same lady into a ditch, just to
get where he is going five seconds sooner.

Sometimes, if I have a premonition of an accident,
I will try to break down, or at least get a flat tire,
so as to cause a delay. It's not always easy to do as
they are making us better and better these days.

I also have to worry about my driver using a cell phone.
My worse yet concern is texting, which gets really scary.
Being owned by a reckless driver is no picnic, but I much
prefer it to being forced into the hectic life of a rental car.

Growing obsolete is nothing to look forward to in any event.
In addition to being allowed to deteriorate, we usually end
up in some country where there are no paved roads and
everyone is aspiring to be a New York City cab driver.

It is no fun not to be loved like we used to be....

My Obedient Finger

I move my finger slowly,
it does what it is told.
It listens to me carefully,
if the truth be known.

If my finger is obedient,
it does what I want it to,
it seems likely my body,
will take instructions too.

The Mind that moves my finger
rules the responsive universe,
I need only trust completely,
for it to honor my requests.

When our mind sends a message to a particular finger which causes it to move, does it obey us as a result of an underlying thought whereby we have initiated an action? Does our finger comply with our wishes being as it has received instructions from our mind? Is the moving of a particular finger an expression of our thoughts? Is it possible we can give ourselves credible suggestions to be, or to remain, in a harmonious state if we realize we have the ability to do so? Would our entire being then become a harmonious expression of our spiritually aligned thoughts? Do our thoughts have creative power?

Does our finger move because it obeys our thought creating mind? If societal beliefs convince us that our finger will no longer respond, will it become unresponsive? Does our mind transmit commands which correspond to our ingrained beliefs, either for our benefit or detriment? Should we deliberate carefully upon the consequences of our thoughts and the resultant subtle directives we are subconsciously creating? Can this be one of the elusive and little understood Truths that sets us free from the burdensome trials of life? Can we demonstrate the courage to hold fast to our firmly held beliefs?

Through the wisdom acquired in contemplative prayer and meditation, we can realize the unreality of the delusion we are continually immersed in. With our unfolding understanding, not only will we be able to give authoritative direction to our obedient finger, we will surely be able to improve the overall quality of our lives. Could the cause of all inharmony be our lack of awareness with regard to our ability to utilize the inherent power of Mind which is flowing directly from the Almighty? When we trust our thoughts have transformational power, we are able to draw upon the infinite reservoir of life and in doing so, we can realize our deepest desires. As a direct result of our trust, coupled with the exalted quality of our thoughts, we are lovingly restored and renewed.

Our Country's Motto

Do you know our country's
motto is "In God We Trust?"
It was to be our guiding principle,
but somehow it has been lost.

Could it be that we are unaware
what our forefathers tried to do?
To instill a sense of trust in God,
regarding all that's right to do?

Did they trust in God to guide us,
long after they were gone?
Did they leave us a reminder
to help us to carry wisely on?

If we all trust in God to guide us,
will our country soon grow strong?
Can we put Him in the forefront,
where He undoubtedly belongs?

Pious Parrot

There was a Pious Parrot,
who quoted scripture night and day.
He was quite well versed
and knew exactly what to say.

He thrived on the attention,
as he would eloquently talk.
Yet if a cat would threaten,
he would worryingly squawk.

He spoke of Daniel's lack of fear,
when he survived the lion's den.
Unlike Daniel, when a cat was near,
his squawk was quite intense.

Pious Parrot was a simple bird,
who did not yet understand.
The truths that he was uttering,
were conceived at God's command.

What he espoused was so profound,
he could barely understand it.
The meaning gradually evolved,
it was as God had planned it.

His trust had grown undaunting,
as he unceasingly declared it.
He no longer will be squawking,
like a frightened Pious Parrot.

Poems of Encouragement

Poems of encouragement are inspirational. Unfortunately, it is detachment from the life that is God that makes our own lives barren and difficult. Truly joyful poems that lift our spirits can oftentimes connect us to nature, love, wisdom, peace and joy, which are all synonymous with God. They speak to us in the voice of God when they have the ring of truth in them.

If you knew for sure that you had the power to demonstrate over every difficulty in your eternal life, would you be afraid of anything ever again? Curiously, this is what the deeper aspects of Christianity, Buddhism, Hinduism and Judaism are trying to convey to us. They seek to confirm the fact that, through knowledge and understanding, we are able to grow to a spiritual level of awareness whereby we can tune in to God's love, power and protection. The divine Mind of God enriches, heals and enlightens us as we utilize our imperishable connection to His unalterable laws of Cause and Effect.

We recognize we are co-creators with God for the benefit of ourselves and others by reason of the fact, "We reap what we sow." These unalterable divine Laws enable us to do our part in creating a better world.

When we have grown spiritually to the degree we intuitively understand that for every action there is a precisely equal reaction, we can intentionally create and thereby use each action and subsequent reaction in a beneficial way. We will have learned to use God's unalterable laws of Cause and Effect in accordance with His will for us, which is always for the best of all involved. We grow to understand our exalted thoughts and actions are actually prayers for humanity and are being brought to fruition in a very demonstrable way.

IMAGE № 14 - Christ's Life Depicted in Art

Jesus Forgives the Sinful Woman.
Drawing by Heinrich Hofmann.

Reflections in a Dreamer's Mirror

I dreamt I peered into a mirror,
God was where I should have been,
He gently reassured me,
"You won't return again."

"Keep looking in the mirror
and I will make it clearer,
about the many times and places
and the dreams that you have lived."

I watched with great amazement,
I saw all that I've been through,
the mirror was revealing,
the countless "me's" for my review.

Each reflection seemed familiar,
as though we were meeting once again.
It was as if I was rediscovering,
all my long lost loving friends.

"Those seekers that you're seeing,
are your past identities.
You've learned to live in harmony,
and now your soul is free."

"The person that you are today,
has learned to use my powers.
You trust that I will see you through,
life's seeming darkest hours."

"You've learned the meaning of the truth,
you were always safe with me.
You have learned to trust me and the truth has set you free."
"Through life's trials and tribulations,
you have found your way to me.
You've earned the right to live your life, with me, eternally."

Seekers

I am a seeker, an immortal soul,
made visible as an incarnate being
laboring for higher consciousness.
I cultivate the garden of experience
and reap the harvest of wisdom.

Much like a hand slips from a glove,
I will shuffle off this mortal coil.
Like a slow and persistent caterpillar
evolves into a magnificent butterfly,
I will ascend beyond time and space.

Understanding acquired here
will spirit me to higher realms.
I will search for love and perfection
with those seekers of truth on the
same sacred journey, united by love.

Photo by Ms. Malgorzata Szlachta

Shakespeare's Sonnet, № 44

an interpretation

If the dull substance of my flesh were thought,
If I were able to project my flesh bound consciousness
into a luminous, thought responsive, ethereal body,

Injurious distance would not bar my way;
We would no longer suffer the pain of separation;

For then despite of space I would be brought,
I could be with you regardless of distance,

To limits far remote where thou dost stay.
I could be wherever you are.

No matter that my foot did stand
Upon the farthest earth removed from thee;
Distance is not a reality on the ethereal plane;

For nimble thought can jump both sea and land
thoughts have no geographical boundaries

As soon as think the place where thou might be
I'd need only think of you to be with you

But ah, thought kills me that I am not thought
I am painfully aware I cannot liberate myself from my physical body

To leap large lengths of miles where thou hast gone
I am unable to enjoy your injuriously distant presence

But that so much of earth and water wrought
while bearing the cumbersome restrictions of this earth plane

I must attend times leisure with my moan
I must pass the lingering time away from you in sorrowful longing

Receiving naught form elements so slow
immediate gratification is not possible as long as I remain bound to my physical body

But heavy tears badge of either's woe
inconsolable sorrow reassures us of the sincerity of our mutual affection

William Shakespeare (1564 – 1616).

An English playwright, poet, and actor, widely regarded as
the greatest writer in the English language and the world.

Soulbird

The Soulbird's cage was open,
but he did not want to leave.
He chose the safety of his confines,
over his desire to be free.

The cage had been his home,
was it all he'd ever known?
Now that it was open,
If he left, where would he go?

The thought of being free,
to explore unfamiliar worlds,
was overshadowed by uncertainty
and fear of the unknown.

The Soulbird could opt
for liberation voluntarily,
or prolong the inevitable,
until he'd be forced to leave.

He made a choice to venture on,
it was one he won't regret.
The cage became unbearable,
he was glad that he had left.

The world beyond the cage,
was quite a sight to see.
The Soulbird was relieved
and was happy to be free.

Sparkling River

Sparkling River shimmering bright,

enfold me in your glistening light.

Let your gentle whispering waves,

inspire pleasant thoughts to save.

Radiant Sun you will soon retreat

departing with your luminous warmth.

Some other day we three shall meet,

for now you both are in my thoughts.

Photo by Paul Martin

Tender Mercies

Soothe me with your tender mercies,
enfold me in your purifying Grace.
Whisper truth within the silence,
keep me safe in your embrace.

Let my thoughts ascend to thee,
with body light and spirit free.
Will you appear and rescue me?
May I dwell in heartfelt harmony?

Your light reflects upon my soul,
the mysteries of life unfold.
Your overflowing love abounds,
your soundless symphony surrounds.

Your flame of Grace enraptures me.
May I never again lose sight of thee?
May I cling to all abiding joy in thee?
May I depend on you for all my needs?

I am speechless, marveling in wonder.
What you reveal is quite profound;
for within your blissful presence,
your tender mercies can be found.

Grant me unshakable courage,
as well as pure unwavering trust.
Let my path of life unfold, with no
fear or doubt, or thoughts of self.

IMAGE № 19 - Christ's Life Depicted in Art

Jesus with Mary and Martha.
Painting by Heinrich Hofmann.

Thank God for Peter

Peter was bidden to walk on water,
He lost faith and so he sank.
Christ reached his hand out to him
and saved him from drowning.

Peter cut off the Centurion's ear
and Christ mercifully restored it so
Peter would not feel so bad about
the terrible thing he had done.

He would deny Christ three times
and knowing this, Christ still declared,
"Upon this rock I will build my church."
Peter learned to have more courage.

Thanks to Peter I am forever reassured,
I am not the only one who makes mistakes.
Christ will reach his hand out to me as well,
as long as I am following in his footsteps.

IMAGE № 16 - Christ's Life Depicted in Art

Jesus and Peter Walk on Water.
Drawing by Heinrich Hofmann.

The Living God

I open my heart to the living God,
giver of all strength and blessings.
He frees me from unworthy thoughts.
He is the source of my inspiration.
From Him comes my joy of safety
when I depend on Him faithfully.
He whispers words of wisdom.
He affirms my divine heritage.
He shelters me and guides me.
He is the living voice of my soul.

He enhances my life according
to the exact expression of my
words, thoughts and actions.
When I raise my expectations to
the magnitude of His love for me,
I am able to overcome what seem
to be insurmountable obstacles.
His power flows through me.
I am sustained and transformed
by His boundlessly loving grace.
I am safe in His loving care and
guidance to the degree I trust in
His compassionate presence.

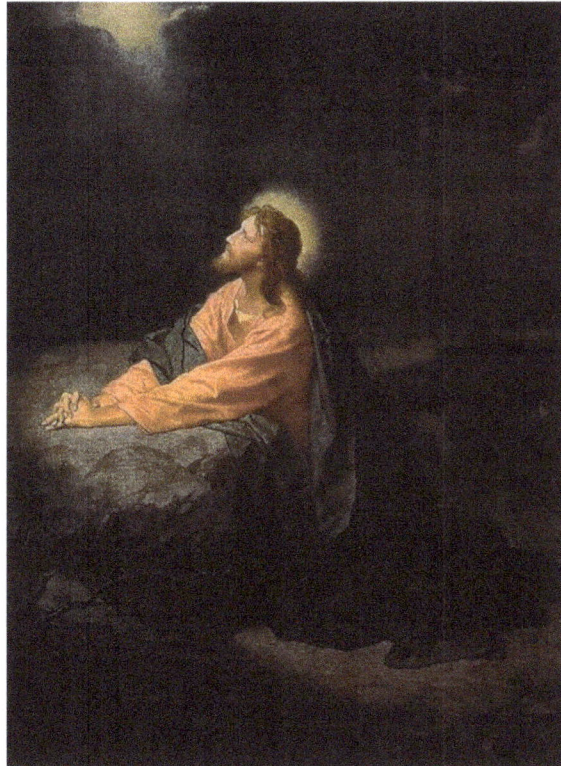

IMAGE № 26 - Christ's Life Depicted in Art

❈

Jesus Praying in the Garden of Gethsemane.
Painting by Heinrich Hofmann.

The Lost Garden of Eden

Union with God, is experiencing God as bliss, love, peace, light, intuition, immortality, and may be achieved through wisdom, morality and dedication to one's evolving illumination. Within the urgent demands of daily life it is required of our immortal souls to find God now. Christ Jesus emphasized the eternal, inseparable relationship between God and his children with the use of the words "Our Father" as he set forth so eloquently in "The Lord's Prayer." In God's beneficence and love all beings can find inner strength, peace, joy and realization. We need only lift the insidious, soul shrouding veil of delusion to be aware of his presence.

To live in the consciousness of God is to be through with enslavement to suffering and fear. To experience the Divine Presence brings happiness into one's life beyond all expectations. Through unfailing devotion we can behold each unfolding drama with the calm joy of life as seen through a lens of immortality. We begin to see eternal life through God's eyes. We realize age and time are non-existent. We become aware we are, and life is, eternal. We rekindle the purity of childhood when we trust that we are secure in God's loving care. The deeper our communion with God the more we transcend the ensnaring web of delusion.

A consistent inner happiness unconditioned by external influence is proof of the responding presence of God and the magnificence of his eternal illumination. God wants us to live our lives as "immortals" so we can remain detached from life's constant roller coaster ride. We intuitively understand, "This too shall pass." When we are ready to leave "this stage of life" we can say with certainty, "Father, this was all very enlightening but now I am ready to come home." By steadfast devotion I have regained the purity of "The Lost Garden of Eden."

IMAGE № 4 - Christ's Life Depicted in Art

❂

The Infant with Mary and Joseph.
Painting by Bartolome Murillo.

The Mortal Dream

We immortal beings co-exist in perfect union with our beloved,
as fully realized and awakened individuals,
neither male nor female,
filled with love, peace, joy and understanding,
never sleeping, eating, desiring, beginning or ending,
sharing boundless, blissful joy and love,
being part of a collective consciousness too vast to imagine,
too perfect to fathom the level of perfection,
enriching and being enriched,
being no more or no less than others,
absolutely and uniquely equal and supremely co-existent.

To remain in this unfathomable union requires absolute humility,
consequently, some of us occasionally suffer the belief that we have fallen out of grace,
we then fall into a deep sleep,. . . we dream we are born into a physical world,
a world in which we have flesh and blood and bodies, gender, parents, siblings,
children, mates, friends, enemies, beginnings and endings, problems and solutions,
we believe we are subject to sickness and pain,
we believe time is a reality,
we believe the greatest illusion of all,
our time will eventually run out and we will someday die,
belief in death is in fact a catalyst for our inevitable reunion,
it is the redeeming influence of our mortal dream,
it is the fear underlying all fears which causes us to search for serenity.

As we think collectively in our oneness with our beloved,
we think collectively in our mortal dream as well.
Most of us believe whatever is popularly accepted by the collective consciousness
with whom we are sharing our mortal dream.
The challenges are constant although not readily apparent,
that which we strongly believe eventually occurs.
Strong beliefs prevail either for our increased awareness or delusion.
We experience much suffering in order to awaken from our mortal dream.
Some of us comprehend the need to awaken before we experience the illusion of death:
if we are able to realize our true spiritual identity we will not fall into a deep sleep
as we did before. . . and dream another mortal dream.
We realize that which we perceive to be reality is actually a dream of mortality.
Some of us have dreamed the mortal dream many times:
all of us will eventually return to our beloved, enriched by our experiences,
ablaze with the love that fueled our burning desire
to reawaken in the state of perpetual amazing grace.

IMAGE № 6 - Christ's Life Depicted in Art

Get thee Behind Me, Satan.
Drawing by Heinrich Hofmann.

The Obligations of Nobility

I am the spirit of nobility.
I have an obligation to uplift humanity
and to uphold the laws of God and man.
I live in the hearts of dedicated people from all walks of life.
I cause them to be kind, considerate, unselfish and thoughtful,
to respect another's confidentiality, and to be aware that
understanding is enhanced by sincerity and patience.

It is I who help them to choose their words more carefully,
to understand the greatest gift is to listen or be listened to,
to consider the feelings of others, to leave things unsaid at times,
to keep in mind that love is nourished with kindness while hurtful
words and actions may be forgiven but not necessarily forgotten.

I instill a sense of fair play and a deep realization that
self interests must be subordinated to the greater good.
I influence them to see the unimportance of winning,
for it is far better to humble one's self before God and man.
I inspire noble hearts to stand up to tyrants as the need arises,
for the powerful must protect the powerless at all costs.
I give them the courage to be true to their deepest beliefs.

I impart the understanding that wisdom is an essential ingredient
of life and is developed, one step at a time, through perseverance.
I create an appreciation of the obligations of honorable, generous
and responsible behavior associated with higher levels of thinking.

I am often handed down, from generation to generation, by people
who are aware of the meaning of respect and concern for others.
I live in the hearts of those who accept the obligations of nobility,
noble and true characters who are predestined to uplift humanity.

IMAGE № 10 - Christ's Life Depicted in Art

✤

Healing the Sick.
Drawing by Heinrich Hofmann.

The Still Small Voice

We must never criticize or find fault with anyone or see evil in any person.
If we do the love in our hearts will grow weak. If we can keep our gaze fixed
on the good side and can rejoice in another's victory or good fortune, or
concernedly sympathize with their misfortune or misguidedness, the blessing
of ever greater Love will come to us. This stream of Love purifies our vision and
we see everything more clearly. This is the presence of God that we invite into
our hearts by faithfully and upwardly monitoring our thoughts and actions.

We can always ask ourselves, what would Jesus think about this?
What would Jesus say?

Then we will be guided by the still small voice within.

IMAGE № 25 - Christ's Life Depicted in Art

❖

The Last Super: "Continue Ye in My Love."
Painting by Carl Bloch.

The Truth About Trust

Absolute, unwavering trust in God is the greatest method of instantaneous healing of body (son of man) and Soul (son of God). A steadfast and growing commitment to arouse and consequently deepen our trust is the highest and most rewarding goal one can aspire to. There is nothing more satisfying than the blissful tranquility of meditating on and expanding upon the Truth, once it is realized. Those who demonstrate Truth through their commitment to the practice of uncompromising trust exert a profound and lasting influence on those others who are avidly seeking to establish a firm belief in God's tender loving care, guidance and protection.

The Truth about trust is, our imperishable Soul, and its various manifestations, is eternally safe in God's loving care and guidance to the degree we believe this to be true. Our uppermost desire should be to continually awaken our ever-blossoming consciousness which is, for the most part, mired in uninformed negativity. Eventually we recognize this unburdening revelation to be the fruit of the soothing balm of trust. The realization that God is always willing to help us is the turning point of eternal life. The everlasting now becomes the jubilant existence it was always meant to be.

The Truth about trust was universally bequeathed to humanity by an orderly succession of enlightened prophets including, but not limited to Jesus, Krishna and Buddha, each of whom possessed and demonstrated the ultimate awakening of the Christ Consciousness in all its effulgence. Their purpose was to inspire us to understand how we may bring to fruition our spiritually aligned hopes and desires by placing our trust in the power emanating from the unwavering rock of Truth.

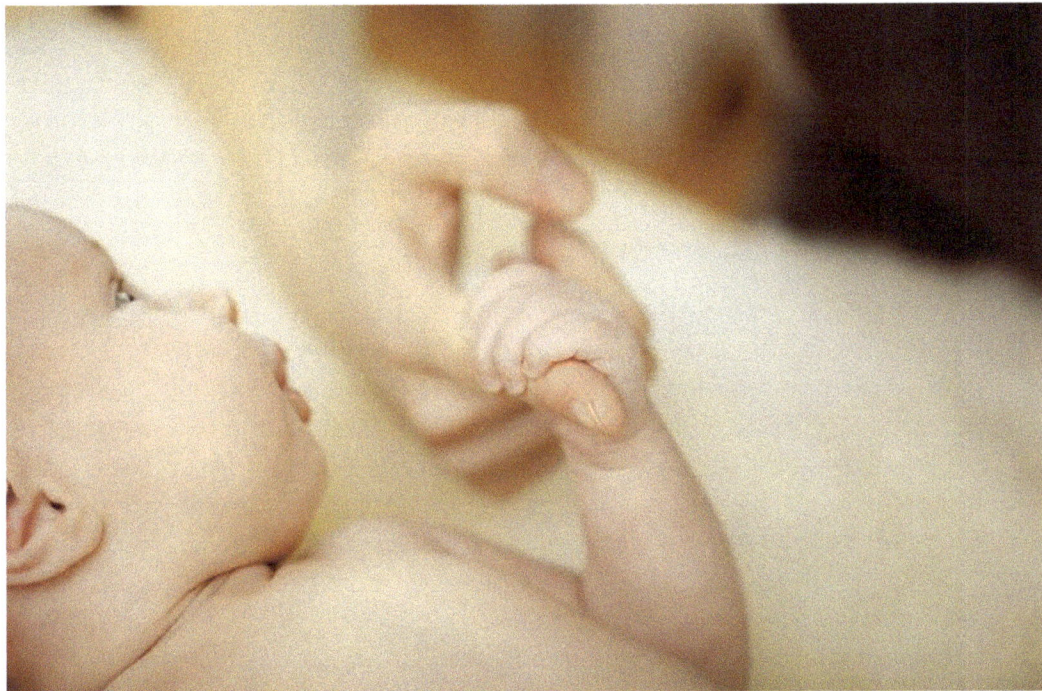

The Turning Point

Like the Sun that slowly rises in the East dispelling the seeming darkness, each of us will eventually realize we are eternally safe in God's loving care. Peace will blossom in us to the degree we understand this phenomenon to be true. Christ Jesus simply said, "you reap what you sow." Did he mean what you believe happens? "We are made in God's image and likeness" and we understand God to be perfect and eternal. Therefore it follows we too are perfect and eternal. We can dispel the beliefs of vulnerability to the painful illusions we are continually exposed to.

Because a cloud hides the Sun, does it mean the Sun does not exist? So it is with omnipotent, omniscient, omnipresent God. Because our erroneous beliefs are blocking us from his love, perfection and protection, does not mean he is not eternally available to protect, correct, guide and love us. It simply means our consciousness has not yet unfolded to this level of spiritual comprehension. Once we realize the perfection of our infinite connection to God our perception of life changes. We become as Christ Jesus counseled us to be, "as little children," safe in our father mother God's loving bosom throughout eternity. We are able to perceive the safety we once felt as little children, the safety born of innocence.

"Thou shalt love the Lord thy God with all thy heart and all thy soul and all thy might and have no false gods before you" simply means that every time we put more faith in a doctor, a medicine, a person, every time we think God is unavailable, in a particular instance, to keep us safe from the hypnotic suggestions of mass thinking, we are violating the first commandment. We are commanded to have implicitly unshakable trust in God. The same God that has the power to heal us also has the power to keep us well. The same God that has the power to see us through tragedy reflects the harmony that can avert tragedy. The same God that created us has the power to protect and guide us throughout eternity. We need only roll back the clouds of erroneous thinking to reveal the magnificent vision of our father mother God who is always beckoning us to come closer, to avail ourselves of his eternal love and protection and to understand our truly magnificent and indestructible selves.

In the realm of God and his eternal permanence time is measured by our unfoldment. This unfoldment is constant and joy filled once we realize we are not vulnerable to the incredible misconceptions of erroneous thought. We need no longer experience suffering in order to grow spiritually. Life becomes the constantly joyous existence it is always meant to be. We have become spiritual beings who have risen above the human experience through the spiritualization of our thoughts. Once acquired, this enlightened understanding is "The turning point of eternal life." We realize "The truth has made us free" from our self-imposed limitations. The Kingdom of Heaven has unfolded in our consciousness.

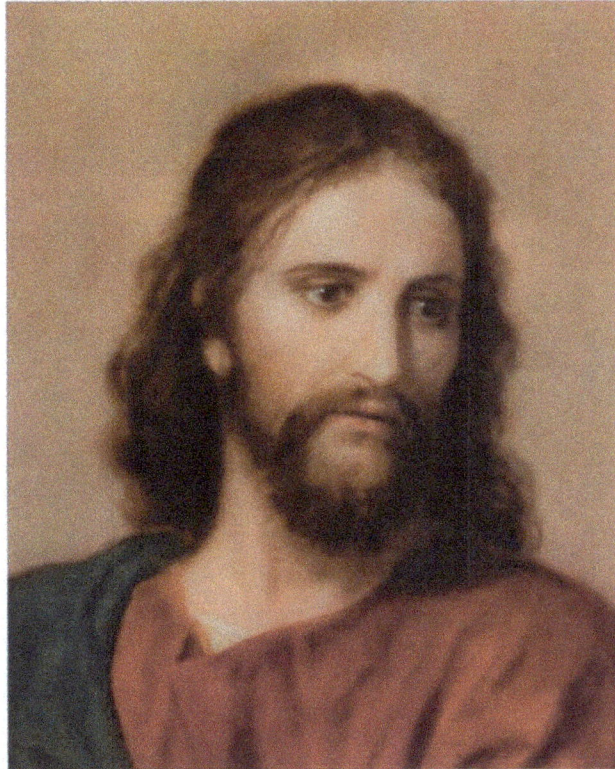

IMAGE № 1 - Christ's Life Depicted in Art

❀

Christ at 33.
Painting by Heinrich Hofmann.
"Lo I am with you alway, even unto the end of the world." - Matthew 28:20

There's A Rolling River

There's a rolling river in your soul,
where you can find what few men know.
There's a fragrant garden in the center of your soul,
where the weak get strong and narrow minds can grow.

Won't you stay with me forever, as we pursue our endless goal,
as we try to find the freedom in the center of our souls.
Don't go away, wish you would stay,
we'll find our way in the center of our souls.

There's a rolling river in your soul,
an eternal giver with a rich and endless flow,
There's a world of love within the center of your soul,
where the rich are rarely seen, but the poor are free to go.

Won't you stay with me forever, as we pursue our endless goal,
as we try to find the freedom in the center of our souls.
Don't go away, wish you would stay,
we'll find our way in the center of our souls.

IMAGE № 20 - Christ's Life Depicted in Art

Christ and the Rich Young Man.
Painting by Heinrich Hofmann.

Truth or Consequences

The Christ Consciousness reflects Spiritual Truth and corresponds perfectly with reality. The kingly Christ intelligence, appointed by the transcendental God to govern all creation is the witness, the reflection of the Truth out of which comes all that exists. Cause and Effect or Karma, as it is known in Eastern Philosophy, is an uncompromising law whereby the consequences of thoughts and actions sown, are reaped precisely in kind.* Therefore, there are no victims. We create the quality of our eternal lives according to what we think and do. Fortunately, there is a remedy to lessen the insidious consequences of limiting negative Karma and to increase the magnanimous blessings of good Karma.

To know the truth about any person, circumstance or condition automatically corrects the circumstance or condition to the extent this truth is understood by the knower. Whenever the Christ imbued Spiritual Truth is raised up in thought with sufficient realization, healing follows, whether it be a physical, moral or intellectual affliction. It makes no difference how difficult a particular problem may appear to be. The actual spiritual truth behind the appearance of an erroneous condition will heal it, being as it will be corrected by no less than the direct action of God himself. The higher laws of Spirit supersede all the lower laws of the physical plane. This surely means that Man, because of his Divine selfhood, has the power to rise above the physical plane into the realm of infinite Spirit where the laws of the lower plane no longer affect him. The laws of the physical plane have not been broken, Man has simply risen above them.

Karmic law gives no preference to anyone, nor does it overlook the slightest occurrence. Fortunately the law governs matter and not Spirit, for in Spirit all is perfect and eternal unchanging Goodness. Here, there is no good or bad karma to be reaped or to be sown. Therefore when Man, through prayer and contemplation, elevates his consciousness to the pure realm of Spirit beyond physical matter,** he comes under the perfect laws of God. Bad Karma is seen to be the surmountable consequences of entrenched erroneous beliefs. The negative consequences of Cause and Effect, the cause of all suffering, are transcended.

This means nothing less than the fact that Karmic debt accumulated by wrong thoughts and actions can be overcome by sufficiently altering the character of Man by means of intuitive perception. As a repentant transgressor becomes more "Christ like," the consequences of his offenses are transcended, being as the Christ Consciousness is the ruler of Cause and Effect. He perceives belief in limitation to be the duplicitous power that creates and sustains it. It is somewhat like light flooding into a darkened room when a switch has been turned on, seekers were stumbling in the darkness simply because they were unable to find the switch. Herein lies the true meaning of Christ coming into the world to redeem and save it. As Man enters the realm of Spirit and is enlightened by the Christ Consciousness, he shall know the Truth and the Truth shall set him free to rise above all limitations. The realization of the Christ Truth is that which tips the scales of Karma in his favor.

 * The Biblical parallel to Cause and Effect a.k.a. Karma is "As you sow, so shall you reap."
** Refer to - "The Mortal Dream" by Paul Martin.

IMAGE № 12 - Christ's Life Depicted in Art

⚜

Driving the Money Changers out of the Temple.
Drawing by Heinrich Hofmann.

We Trust in God's Eternally Sheltering Love & Guidance

This insight represents the essence of spirituality and embodies the spirit of Christ's teachings.

"We" signifies humanity as being all of God's children created equally and equally loved.

"Trust" is the essential ingredient of faith, the cornerstone of hope and the process of spiritual evolution by which we progress from blind faith and baseless hope to spiritual conviction gained through understanding. When we trust in God's eternally sheltering love and guidance we take comfort in his infinite protection. We lift the veil of delusion that separates us from the peace and joy of God within us. To be sheltered and protected from life's continual onslaughts is an immeasurable blessing. To be eternally guided through prayerfully acquired and magnanimously bestowed intuition is to find solace in the God-given awarenesses that allow us to navigate the often treacherous and unchartered waters of life. We are able to gravitate effortlessly toward the peace and serenity of His sheltering love. Whoever wholeheartedly desires the tender protection of Almighty God will be unceasingly enlightened by the infinite wisdom of divinely granted intuition.

IMAGE № 24 - Christ's Life Depicted in Art

The Last Super: "And He Took The Cup . . ."
Drawing by Heinrich Hofmann.

Poem & Prayer   The Best of www.MyPrayers.net

What Does God Look Like?

A child was working feverishly on a portrait in her pre-school art class.

Her teacher inquired, "What are you drawing?"

The little girl replied, "I am drawing God."

The teacher replied, "Please don't be upset but that is not possible because no one knows what God looks like."

The child replied without hesitation,

"They will in a minute."*

The moral of the story is in order to know God and commune with Him, we must have childlike trust in His eternal Love and guidance. We see God when we possess the simple loving nature of a child.

©7/20/2016 Paul Martin. All rights reserved.
What Does God Look Like?   www.MyPrayers.net

* Adapted from India Folklore.

128

What is Truth?

Truth is the absolute, intelligent and principled nature of God and is demonstrated through his unalterable laws of Cause and Effect. Love, Grace and Goodness flow from this one divine source. Truth manifests itself in many different ways as it either rewards or corrects us according to our understanding of and adherence to God's spiritual laws. Truth is in exact correspondence with reality and is uncontaminated by mankind's mindless, self-serving rationalizations. It is the expression of God's perfect government of all that exists. We are empowered by God to multiply the blessings in our lives by monitoring our every thought and action to be sure we are expressing Love and compassion. To feel Love is to feel the presence of Truth. To feel the absence of Love is to feel the absence of Truth. We all eventually realize the love we receive is precisely equal to the love we give. We create a harmonious life by demonstrating Truth on a moment to moment basis.

Truth is synonymous with:

absolute, all-knowing, allness, almighty, attunement, awareness, blessings, bliss, candor, cause and effect, Christ, comforting, communion, compassion, consciousness, consideration, creativity, dawn, definite, devotion, divine law, divine order, Divinity, enlightenment, equality, ethical, ethics, experience, fairness, faith, faithful, faultless, forbearance, forgiveness, freedom, friendship, glory, God, God's Will, goodness, happiness, harmony, healing, healthy, help, honesty, honor, humility, identity, illumination, immaculate, immortality, indisputable, infinite, innocence, inspiration, integrity, intelligence, intuition, irreversible, joy, joyful, karma, kind, kindness, liberation, Life, light, like, living, Love, meditation, metaphysical, metaphysics, Mind, morality, nature, nobility, omnipotence, omnipresence, omniscience, oneness, order, patience, peace, peaceful, perception, perfect, perfection, philosophical, philosophy, praiseworthy, prayer, Principle, pristine, pure, purity, reality, realization, reflection, reliable, resolute, respect, resurrection, revelation, righteousness, sacred, Savior, science, Self, selflessness, simplicity, Soul, Spirit, spirituality, sublime, Substance, supernatural, supreme, The Word, transcendental, trust, unalterable, unbounded, unconditional, unconditional love, understanding, union, united, universal, unprejudiced, veracity, verity, virtue, vision, whole, wisdom, worthy, Yoga.

IMAGE № 11 - Christ's Life Depicted in Art

The Sermon on the Mount.
Painting by Carl Bloch.

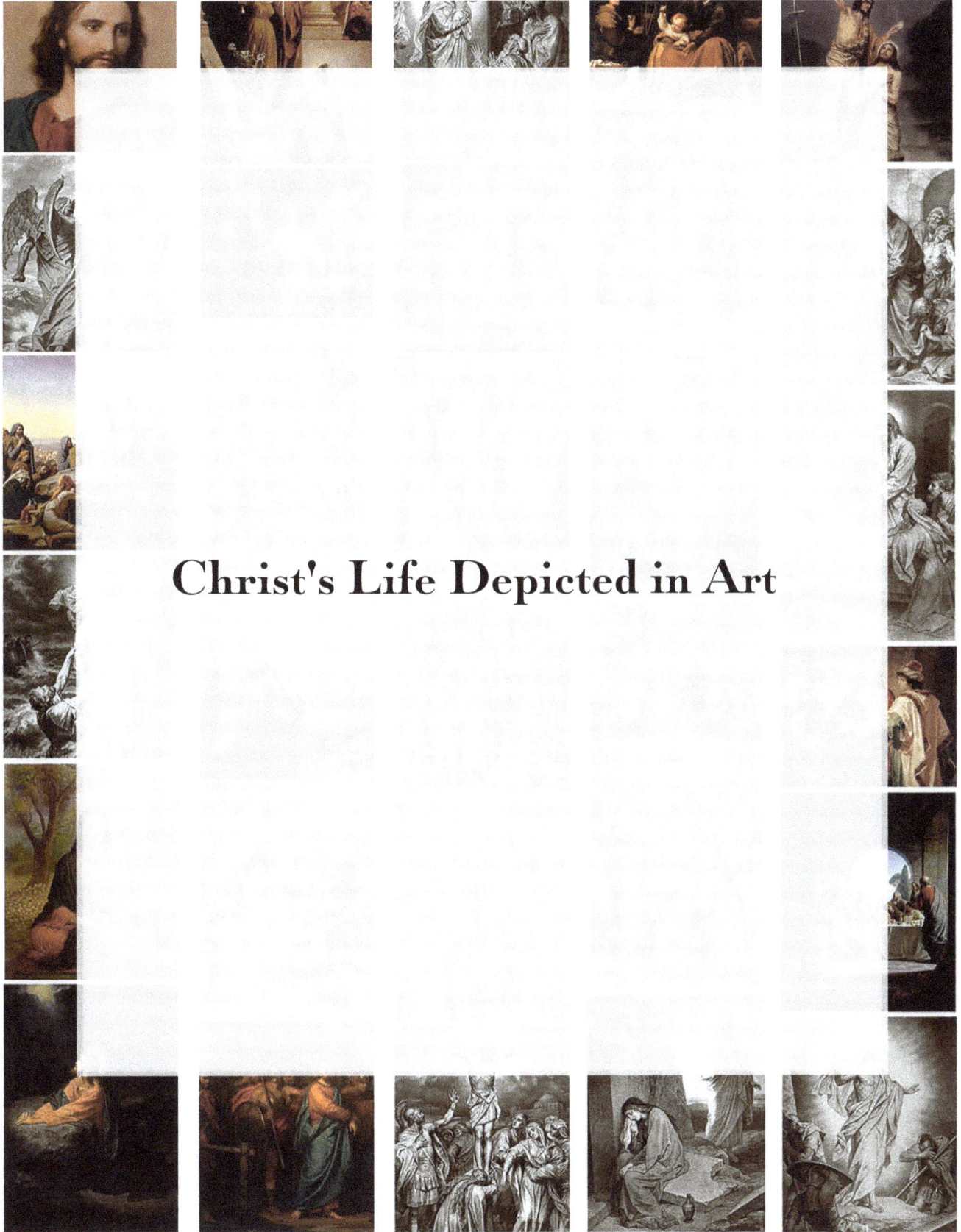

Christ's Life Depicted in Art

Christ at 33

IMAGE № 1

Painting by Heinrich Hofmann.
"Lo I am with you alway, even unto the end of the world." - Matthew 28:20

Mary Visits the Mother of John the Baptist

IMAGE № 2

Painting by Carl Heinrich Bloch.
Courtesy of Det Nationalhistoriske Museum på Frederiksborg, Hillerød, Denmark.

The Visit of the Three Wise Men

IMAGE № 3

Drawing by Heinrich Hofmann.

The Infant With Mary and Joseph

IMAGE № 4

Painting by Bartolome Murillo.

The Baptism of Jesus

IMAGE № 5

Painting by Carl Heinrich Bloch.
Courtesy of Det Nationalhistoriske Museum på Frederiksborg, Hillerød, Denmark.

Get thee Behind Me, Satan

IMAGE № 6

Drawing by Heinrich Hofmann.

The Boy Jesus with the Doctors in the Temple

IMAGE № 7

Painting by Heinrich Hofmann.

The Childhood of Jesus

IMAGE № 8

Drawing by Heinrich Hofmann.

Jesus and the Woman of Samaria

IMAGE № 9

Drawing by Heinrich Hofmann.

Healing the Sick

IMAGE № 10

Drawing by Heinrich Hofmann.

The Sermon on the Mount

IMAGE № 11

Painting by Carl Heinrich Bloch.
Courtesy of Det Nationalhistoriske Museum på Frederiksborg, Hillerød, Denmark.

Driving the Money Changers out of the Temple

IMAGE № 12

Drawing by Heinrich Hofmann.

The Woman Taken in Adultery

IMAGE № 13

Drawing by Heinrich Hofmann.

Jesus Forgives the Sinful Woman

IMAGE № 14

Drawing by Heinrich Hofmann.

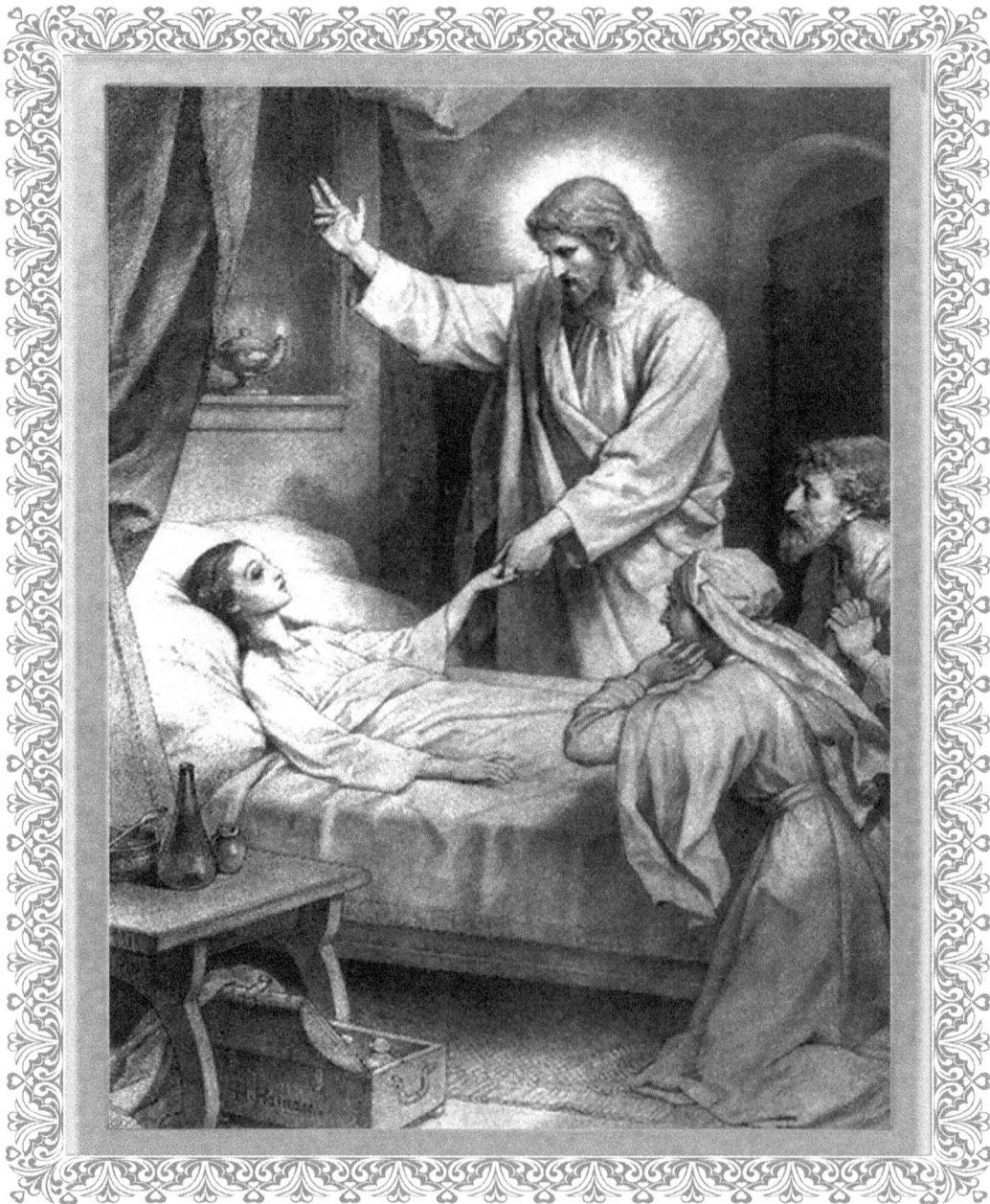

Jesus Raises Jairus's Daughter From the Dead

IMAGE № 15

Drawing by Heinrich Hofmann.

Jesus and Peter Walk on Water

IMAGE № 16

Drawing by Heinrich Hofmann.

The Transfiguration

IMAGE № 17

Painting by Carl Heinrich Bloch.
Courtesy of Det Nationalhistoriske Museum på Frederiksborg, Hillerød, Denmark.

Become as Little Children

IMAGE № 18
❁

Drawing by Heinrich Hofmann.

Christ with Mary and Martha

IMAGE № 19

Painting by Heinrich Hofmann.
Courtesy of Stadtmuseum Bautzen, Germany.

Christ and the Rich Young Ruler

IMAGE № 20

Painting by Heinrich Hofmann.
Courtesty of The Riverside Church, New York City and New York Graphic Society.

Jesus in the Interiorization of Prayer in Meditation

IMAGE № 21

❀

Painting by V. V. Sapar.

Suffer the Little Children to Come Unto Me

IMAGE № 22

Drawing by Heinrich Hofmann.

Jesus' Entry into Jerusalem

IMAGE № 23

Drawing by Heinrich Hofmann.

The Last Super: "And He Took the Cup..."

IMAGE № 24

Drawing by Heinrich Hofmann.

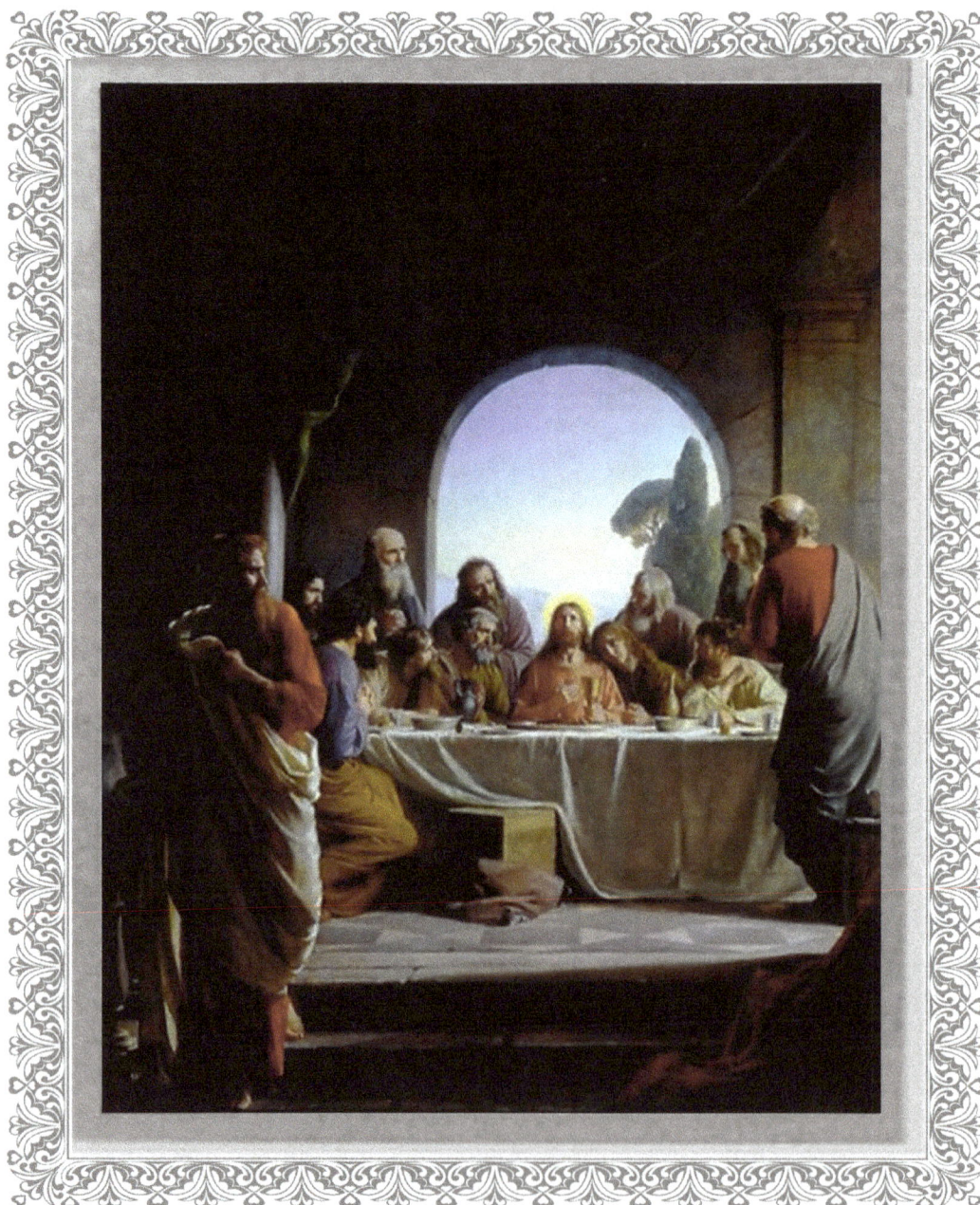

The Last Super: "Continue Ye in My Love."

IMAGE № 25

Painting by Carl Heinrich Bloch.
Courtesy of Det Nationalhistoriske Museum på Frederiksborg, Hillerød, Denmark.

Jesus Praying in the Garden of Gethsemane

IMAGE № 26

Painting by Heinrich Hofmann.
Courtesty of The Riverside Church, New York City and New York Graphic Society.

The Arrest of Jesus

IMAGE № 27

Painting by Heinrich Hofmann.
Courtesy of Hessisches Landesmuseum Darmstadt, Germany.

The Crucifixion

IMAGE № 28

Drawing by Heinrich Hofmann.
"Lo I am with you alway, even unto the end of the world." - Matthew 28:20

Jesus with Mary Magdalene at the Tomb

IMAGE № 29

Drawing by Heinrich Hofmann.

The Resurrection

IMAGE № 30

Drawing by Heinrich Hofmann.

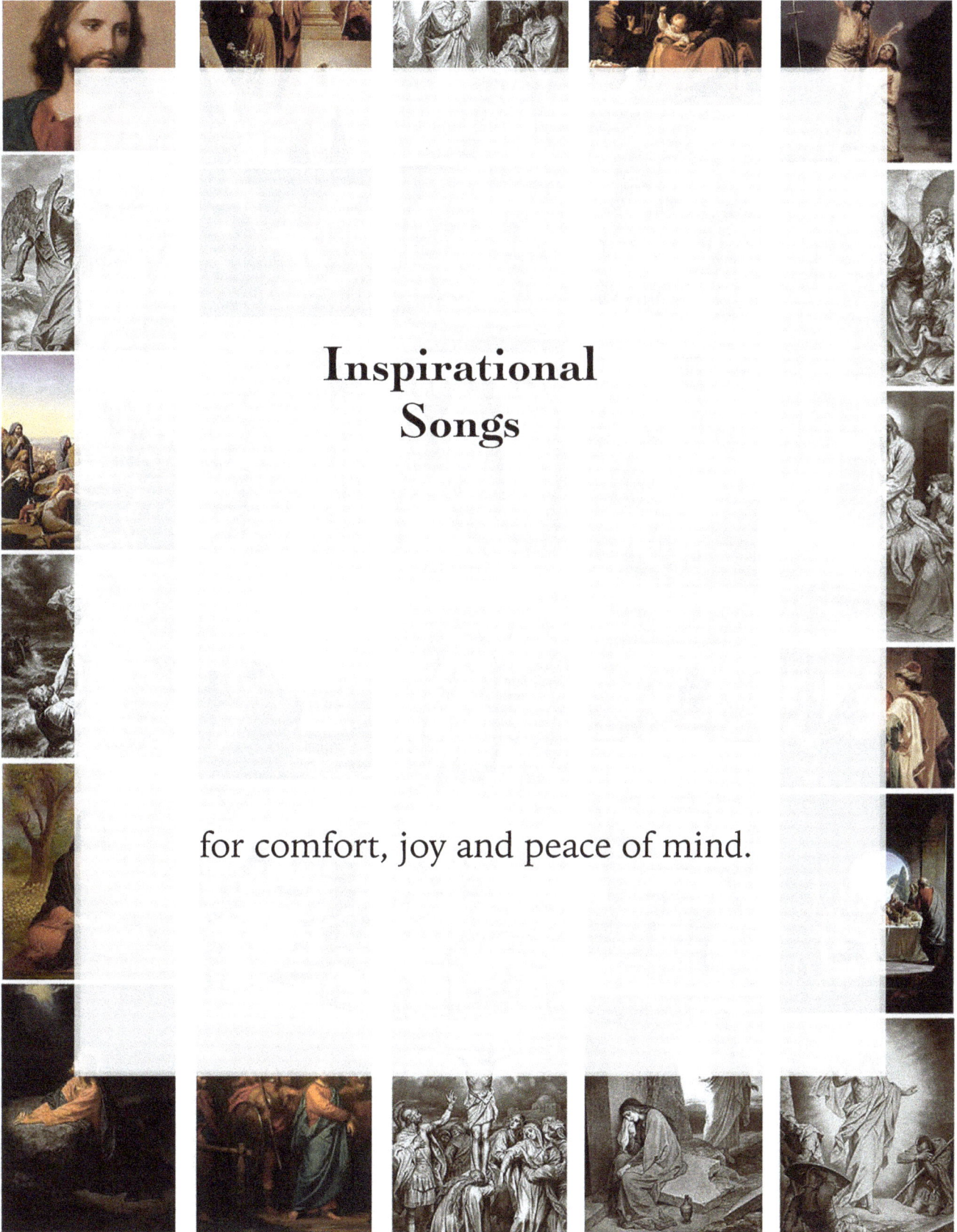

Inspirational
Songs

for comfort, joy and peace of mind.

Amazing Grace

Amazing grace! How sweet the sound,
that saved and set me free!
I once was lost, but now am found,
was blind, but now I see.

It was grace that taught my heart to care,
and grace my fears relieved;
How precious did that grace appear,
the hour I first believed!

Through many dangers, toils and snares,
I have already come;
It's grace that's brought me safe thus far,
and grace will lead me home.

The Lord has promised life to me,
in His word I am secure;
He will my guide and shelter be,
for now and ever more.

When this earthly temple fails,
and mortal life shall cease;
I shall possess, beyond the veil,
a life of joy and peace.

When we've been there ten thousand years,
bright shining as the sun;
We've no less days, to sing God's praise,
then when we first begun.

The Baptism of Jesus.
Painting by Carl Bloch.

The lyrics to Amazing Grace were written by a preacher named John Newton and were first published in 1779. It was later combined with William Walker's music to a song called New Britain in 1829. The last of the six verses was written by Harriet Beecher Stowe and appeared in her widely acclaimed anti-slavery novel Uncle Tom's Cabin which was published in 1852. Over the years there were some 50 odd verses which have been published in various forms. What I have done is use four of the most popular verses, more specifically verses 1, 2, 3 and 6 and modified them a bit. I also added the lesser known verses 4 and 5 with revisions as well. I have minimally substituted more contemporary words in order to make the entire lyric reflect a truer understanding of the author's intent. I have also created new, different and complementary music for the introduction, verse 3, the musical break, verse 6 and the finale as well.

Over the centuries the truer message has most often been lost sight of. The reality is it was meant to be a happy song about the unexpected acquiring of the realization that life is eternal and we are eternally safe in God's loving care and guidance. I have endeavored to make the entire song reflect more of the joy it was originally intended to convey. It will have a different meaning to some than others depending upon the degree of their own spiritual evolution. Yet, whenever it is performed, it never fails to unite the audience with a common bond of peace and tranquility it has always had the power to engender. To this day it remains one of the most popular, often recorded and/or performed songs ever written.

by Paul Martin

Music Credits
Original lyrics by John Newton and modified by Paul Martin.
Verse 6 written by Harriet Beecher Stowe.
Original music written by William Walker.

℗2012 New music and words written and performed
by Paul Martin.
Produced and arranged by Paul Martin and Daryl Kojak.

℗2013 Lyrics and Music amended by Paul Martin.
Produced and arranged by Paul Martin and Daryl Kojak.

Angels in Our Lives

Could it be someone you idolize, is an unknown Angel in disguise,
from the moment you looked in their eyes, have you had a better life?
As I am growing more aware, it becomes increasingly more clear,
when someone needs an Angel, one will suddenly appear.

When Angels in our lives appear, very little can compare,
to the love and inspiration and the blessings that they bear.
When we find a special friend, is it possible they are heaven-sent,
could it be we are enchanted by their tender love and care?

Have they come to help us find, greater love and peace of mind,
have there been other Angels who have come into your life?
Do you remember every one? Do you know where they have gone?
When they are no longer needed, are they likely to move on?

So look for Angels in your life and I'm sure you will always find,
you will know them by their kindness and love for all mankind.
They won't be wearing angel wings or doing supernatural things,
they are ordinary people, just the same as you and I.

A delightful Angel in our lives will inspire us to desire,
the insight that is needed to find the love we all require.
If they ever go away, we will see them all again someday,
especially when we hope and pray for Angels in our lives.

Music Credits
℗2015 Lyrics and music written and performed by Paul Martin.
Produced and arranged by Paul Martin and Daryl Kojak.

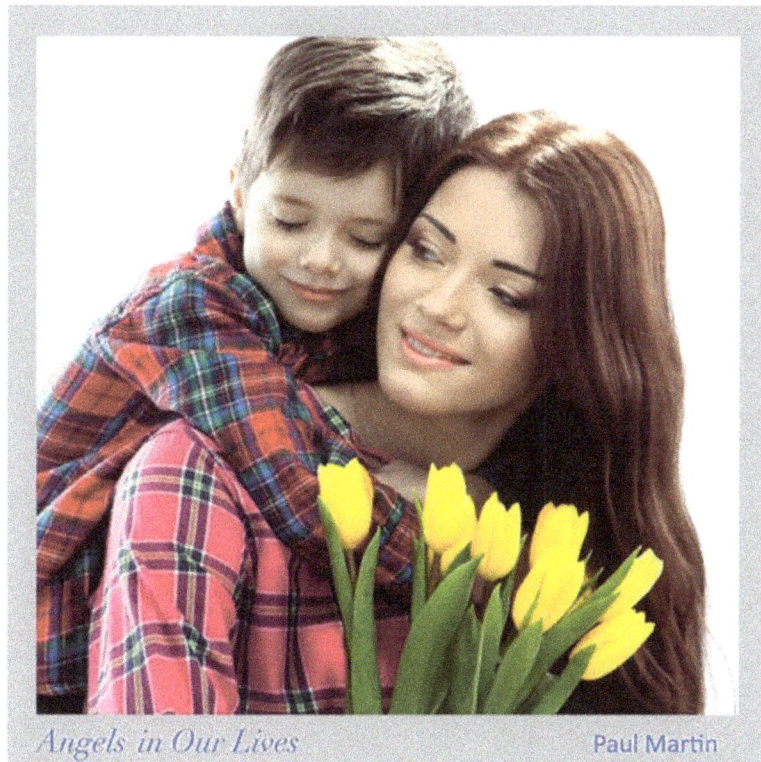

Angels in Our Lives   Paul Martin

Best Old Friends

People come and go, so there is something we should know,
life is better when we're together with our favorite Old Friends.
Throughout all the years, through happiness and tears,
we are helping one another, expecting nothing in return.

Reliving moments from the past, making memories last,
remembering and treasuring pleasures we have shared.
As we meet each other's needs, we wholeheartedly agree,
life is better when we're together with our favorite Old Friends.

Old Friends accept each other
and it doesn't matter when,
the last time we saw each other,
we'll still be best Old Friends.

Can time be better spent, than by being with Old Friends,
we're loyal to each other, like brothers 'til the end.
There may come a time when Old Friends are left behind,
then we'll have our memories to linger in our minds.

I cherish my Old Friends and every now and then,
I have to overlook their ec-cen-tric-i-ties,
I just let them be and hope that they will see,
preserving my old friendships is what matter's most to me.

Old Friends accept each other
and it doesn't matter when,
the last time we saw each other,
we'll still be best Old Friends.

Music Credits
℗2013 Lyrics written and music composed and performed by Paul Martin.
Produced and arranged by Paul Martin and Daryl Kojak.

Upon meeting, Helen Keller
explores Charlie Chaplin's face.

Cherish

Cherish love and cherish flowers,
cherish peace and happy hours,
cherish favorite places we wish we could stay.

Cherish heartfelt music playing,
cherish cheerful little sayings,
cherish counting blessings all throughout the day.

Cherish tales with happy endings,
cherish time that is worth spending,
cherish memories of those who've gone away.

Cherish joy replacing sorrow,
cherish all our bright tomorrows,
that we are looking forward to today.

Cherish truth and cherish kindness,
cherish who and what reminds us,
to seek peacefulness and blessings from above.

Cherish goodness overflowing,
and the happiness of knowing,
our best old friends will fill our hearts with love.

Cherish wisdom we're receiving,
cherish those who are believing,
we are safe in our creator's loving care,

Cherish love and cherish living,
cherish gifts and cherish giving,
all the blessings in our lives we have to share.

Music Credits
℗2014 Lyrics written and music composed and performed by Paul Martin.
Produced and arranged by Paul Martin and Daryl Kojak.

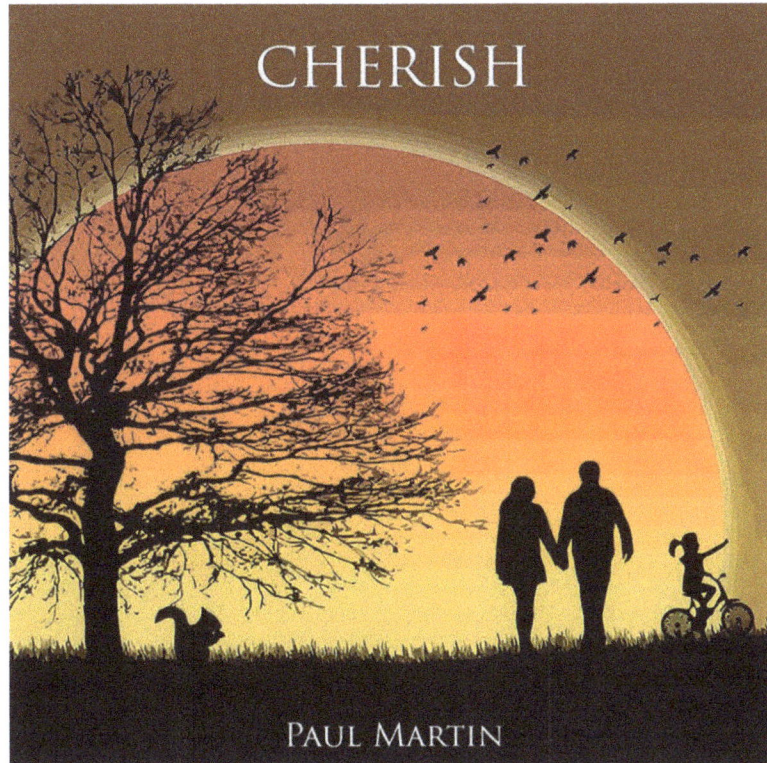

CHERISH

Paul Martin

Child I Will Cherish You

Child I will cherish you as long as you may need me,
I will help you build your dreams and that will truly please me.
You may be just what you want to be and all I ask of you,
whatever you decide it is do it the best that you can do.
And I'd like to see you try, because I cherish you my child.

Little child you are teaching me too,
how often you've reminded me of things that I once knew.
I want to share your happiness I want to share your joy,
You have the power to make me feel like I'm a little boy.
And I'd like to tell you why, because I cherish you my child.

Child I will cherish you, I'll be there when you need me,
Yet I know well that we may not be always in agreement.
I'll help you realize there are times when life may hurt you.
If you can bring yourself to smile, love will not desert you child.
And I'd like to see you try, because I cherish you my child.

Child I will cherish you and someday you won't need me.
This will break my heart and yet this will truly please me.
Knowing that you need me not, it won't be very easy.
Yet I will draw myself aside, content that you don't need me child.
And I'd like to tell you why, because I cherish you my child.

Music Credits
℗1986 Lyrics and music written and performed by Paul Martin.
Produced and arranged by Paul Martin and Jeff Lin.

Image № 22 - Christ's Life Depicted in Art

❧

Suffer the Little Children to Come Unto Me.
Drawing by Heinrich Hofmann.

Do Souls Have Colors, Daddy?

"Do Souls have colors Daddy?"
a child was heard to say.
When someone goes to heaven,
does their color stay the same?

Does each different color Soul
go to a different color place.
Is it likely Souls in heaven,
are separated in this way?

Will Souls have nationalities,
or do they leave them all behind?
Do they speak in different languages,
will Souls alike be hard to find?

Sad Souls whose hearts are bound to
those, from whom they've had to part.
Will God relieve their suffering,
will He mend their broken hearts?

Can Souls be men or women,
is it possible to choose?
Will they stay forever young,
will they continue to improve?

My child, her caring father said,
I'm sure our Souls are all alike,
they're colorless and genderless
and are all equal in God's eyes.

Relationships are different there,
Love is true, like Best Old Friends.
and everyone is very happy,
just to be with God again.

Music Credits
℗2014 Lyrics written and music composed and performed by Paul Martin.
Produced and arranged by Paul Martin and Daryl Kojak.

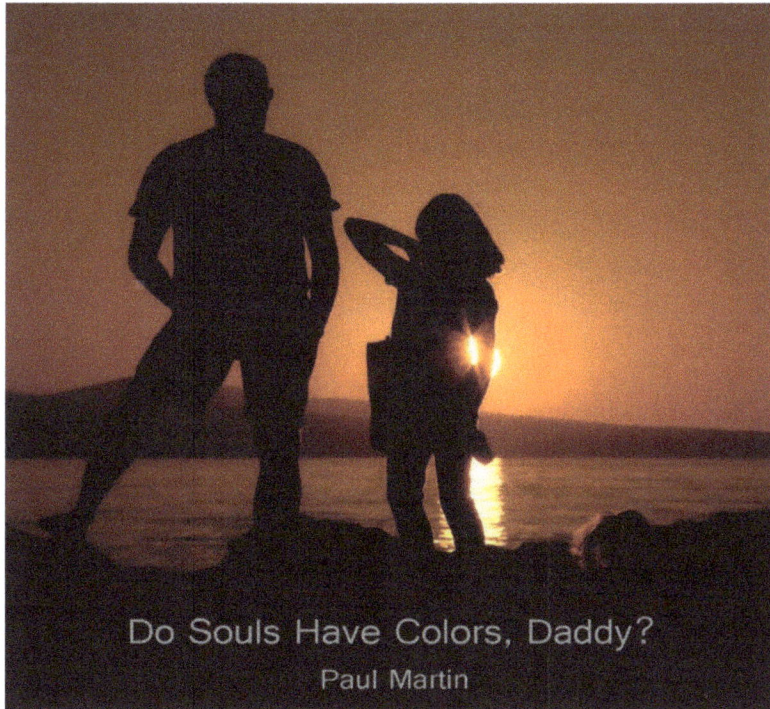

Do Souls Have Colors, Daddy?
Paul Martin

Dreaming Wide Awake

She was dreaming wide awake and she had broken through the barriers to her soul,
She was walking on a tightrope and there were no nets around to break her fall,
She was actress, singer, dancer, poet and was spinning webs of pictures in my mind,
She was dreaming wide awake and the creations of her dreams had come alive.

She was dreaming wide awake I was enchanted by her voice and by her smile,
Her overflowing words were flying much too fast I felt just like a child,
She would sit and stare at me and touch my face as though that she were blind,
She was dreaming wide awake and the artist in me understood her kind.

I watched her very carefully while she was spinning strange and precious lies,
She often did not answer but held my hand and looked into my eyes,
She had a way of being that I never had and never could have been,
I was a willing piece of paper and was receiving my most beautiful imprint.

She was dreaming wide awake I was enchanted by her voice and by her smile,
Her overflowing words were flying much too fast I felt just like a child,
She would sit and stare at me and touch my face as though that she were blind,
She was dreaming wide awake and the artist in me understood her kind.

Music Credits
℗Lyrics and music written and performed by Paul Martin ©1985.
Arrangement and accompaniment by "bluegrass great" Jules Hanson on the guitar.

The Angel's Message.
Painting by George Hillyard Swinstead (1816 - 1890).
George studied at North London School of Art
and at the Royal Academy Schools.

God's Love

I am always with you,
even when you seem unable to feel my presence.
I love you always,
I surround you with my protecting love,
even when you occasionally forget me.
I hear your prayers and answer those that are in
the best interest of all involved including, but not limited to, you.
In me is the unfolding of eternal life's mysteries,
If you are sincere and receptive, I progressively unfold these mysteries to you.

I am the light that illumines your thoughts.
Mine is the sight through which you see.
I am the feeling of love, peace and joy in you.
In me you live and have your being.
I am always at work in your life for your greater good,
although you may not always believe this.
Hopefully, your faith in me will grow constant and
you will discover the secret of opening yourself to my love:
The greater your trust in me the more I am able to fill you with my love.

I want you to give love and equally as important, I want you to receive love.
How else will you learn to love me?
How will you learn to accept my love?
If you injure one of my children you have injured me.
The moment you realize the error of your ways:
The moment you truly regret your wrongdoing,
I forgive you; I nourish you with my tender mercies.

I am aware of your every thought and action as you strive to live in harmony
with my unalterable laws of cause and effect.
Turn to me as you faithfully monitor your thoughts and actions and
I'll grant you the wisdom to treat others as you would have them treat you.
You will discover the love you receive is precisely equal to the love you give.

Eventually you will realize the love I bestow on you through others
is purposefully designed to draw you closer to me.
It is only I who loves you unconditionally.
I am an ever-flowing fountain of love, light, peace and joy.
I will never disappoint you; I will always be with you.
Remember, I never stop loving you for you are my precious child.

Music Credits
℗2012 Music composed by Paul Martin. Music produced and arranged by Paul Martin and Daryl Kojak.

Image № 29 - Christ's Life Depicted in Art

❖

Jesus with Mary Magdalene at the Tomb.
Drawing by Heinrich Hofmann.

God's Will

God's will for us is only good,
perfect body, mind and soul.
To partake of His perfection,
we must disavow the world.

God does not cause suffering
and it's important that we see,
our problems are created
by our erroneous beliefs.

If we know God's will protects us,
we'll be untroubled and serene.
We must trust His will is only good
and His power reigns supreme.

When we absorb the blissful current
of our inner Light, when it appears,
we will realize God empowers us,
as we grow progressively aware.

When we pray, "Thy will be done"
and we surrender, as we should,
we must trust in God's protection
and believe His will is only good.

If we know God's will protects us,
we'll be untroubled and serene.
We must trust His will is only good
and His power reigns supreme.

Music Credits
℗2015 Lyrics and music written and performed by Paul Martin.
Produced and arranged by Paul Martin and Daryl Kojak.

IMAGE № 11 - Christ's Life Depicted in Art

The Sermon on the Mount.
Painting by Carl Bloch.

Home is Where the Heart Is

They say home is where the heart is
and I do believe it's true.
Where the people that I love live,
I would like to live there too.

When I think of far off places,
they don't mean a thing to me.
I need the love and smiley faces,
of my friends and family.

Now I do believe that
dreams can all come true.
My home is where my heart is
and my heart's with all of you.

Home is where my heart is,
I won't stray too far away.
I have a home I am a part of
and I am grateful for each day.

Life is sweet and love is tender,
greater peace I've never known
and I always will remember,
there is no place like home.

Music Credits
℗2015 Lyrics and music written and performed by Paul Martin.
Produced and arranged by Paul Martin and Daryl Kojak.

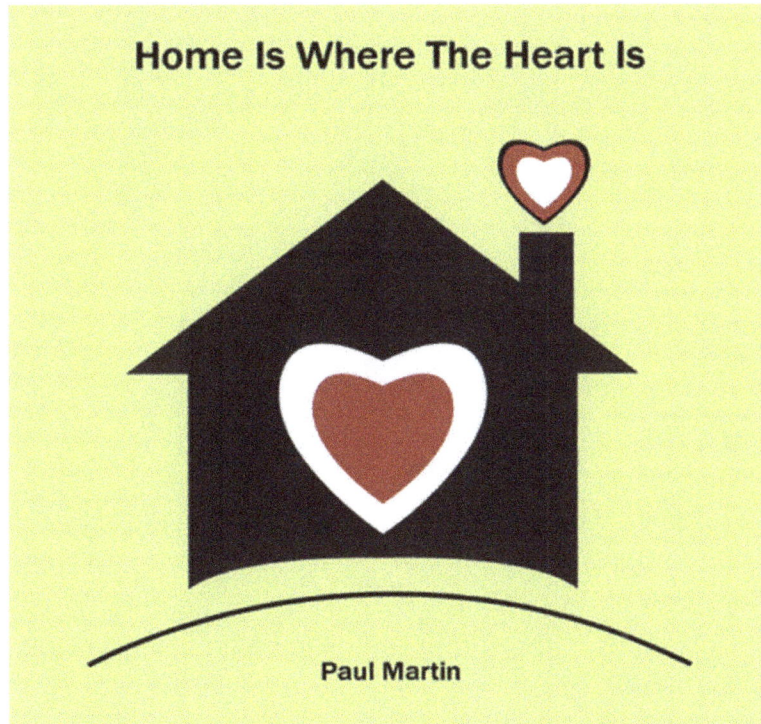

Home Is Where The Heart Is

Paul Martin

I Found You Friend

At times when I lose my spiritual connection to God
I know I can always find Him in the eyes of a friend.

Lost my soul and I couldn't find it anywhere,
looked for God he was nowhere to be found.
Searched in vain but I couldn't find love anywhere,
Then one day heaven opened up its door.

Was then I found you friend and I found what I was looking for,
for it is in your eyes I see the portals of your soul.
And when God thinks of me it is you he sends to help me,
and when he smiles on me it's through you that I am told.

Friends are those we love and trust and cherish,
friends are those we hold close to our hearts.
Friends are those who love and care and nourish,
friends are those whose souls will never part.

O yes I found you friend and I found what I was looking for,
for it is in your eyes I see the portals of your soul.
And when God thinks of me it is you he sends to help me,
and when he smiles on me it's through you that I am told.

Music Credits
℗Lyrics and music written and performed by Paul Martin ©1984.
Produced and arranged by Paul Martin and Dave Kumin.

Painting by George Bernard O'Neill (1828 – 1917).
A prolific Irish genre painter
and a member of the Cranbrook Colony of artists.

I'll Get Through It Every Time

Some say they've seen the other side
and there's nothing to compare,
to the peace and joy and happiness,
that's waiting for us there.

When the burdens of this world,
weigh heavy on my mind,
I look up to the heavens and
I get through it every time.

I'll get through it every time,
there's no mountain I can't climb.
When it's meant to be, eventually
everything will work out fine.

Whatever problems may arise,
will be a blessing in disguise,
I trust that God will help me
to get through it every time.

Should life becomes unpleasant
and peace be hard to find.
I'll count my many blessings
and I'll get through it every time.

I am a cherished child of God
and He is always on my mind.
I trust that He will help me,
to get through it every time.

I'll get through it every time,
there's no mountain I can't climb.
When it's meant to be, eventually
everything will work out fine.

Whatever problems may arise,
will be a blessing in disguise,
I trust that God will help me
to get through it every time.

Music Credits
℗2014 Lyrics written and music composed and performed by Paul Martin.
Produced and arranged by Paul Martin and Daryl Kojak.

IMAGE № 30 - Christ's Life Depicted in Art

The Resurrection.
Drawing by Heinrich Hofmann.

I'll Make Your Life A Little Easier

I'll make your life a little easier,
I'll be considerate and kind.
I will lift life's burdens from you,
I will give you peace of mind.

I will make your life a little easier,
and if you do the same for me.
We'll be helping one another,
it's the way that life should be.

The things we say and do,
and the kindness that we show.
Make life a little easier,
as you and I both know.

Is there a way that I can help you,
Is there something I can do.
To make your life a little easier,
Is what I'd like to do for you.

I'll make your life a little easier,
and I do believe it's true.
If I should ever need you,
you will want to help me too.

The things we say and do,
and the kindness that we show.
Make life a little easier,
as you and I both know.

I'll make your life a little easier,
I'll be considerate and kind.
I will lift life's burdens from you,
I will give you peace of mind.

Music Credits
℗2013 Lyrics written and music composed and performed by Paul Martin.
Produced and arranged by Paul Martin and Daryl Kojak.

IMAGE № 9 - Christ's Life Depicted in Art

Jesus and the Woman of Samaria.
Drawing by Heinrich Hofmann.

I'm Going Home For Christmas

Christmas day is coming, I am happy and I'm humming,
Merry Christmas songs.
Frosty snowflakes are falling, as I spend my time calling,
all my friends back home.

Christmas bells are ringing and the happy children singing,
takes me way back when,
I'd count the days to remind me, that another day's behind me,
'til I'm home for Christmas once again.

I'm going home for Christmas,
I wish that I were there again.
On top of my Christmas wish list,
is my family and friends.

I know what I am missing, it's the hugging and the kissing,
til I'm home again.
Anxiously I'm waiting, I can't help anticipating,
being home for Christmas once again.

Christmas trees are decorated, I'm impatient and elated,
to be going home.
Frosty snowmen are appearing and I'm happy to be hearing,
Merry Christmas songs.

Christmas cheer is abounding and the carolers are sounding,
just like long lost friends.
I sing along to remind me, that another day's behind me.
'til I'm home for Christmas once again.

I'm going home for Christmas,
I wish that I were there again,
On top of my Christmas wish list,
is my family and friends.

Soon I will be sharing all the happiness and caring,
when I'm home again.
Anxiously I am waiting, I can't help anticipating,
being home for Christmas once again.

Music Credits
℗2012 Lyrics and music written and performed by Paul Martin. Produced and arranged by Paul Martin and Daryl Kojak.

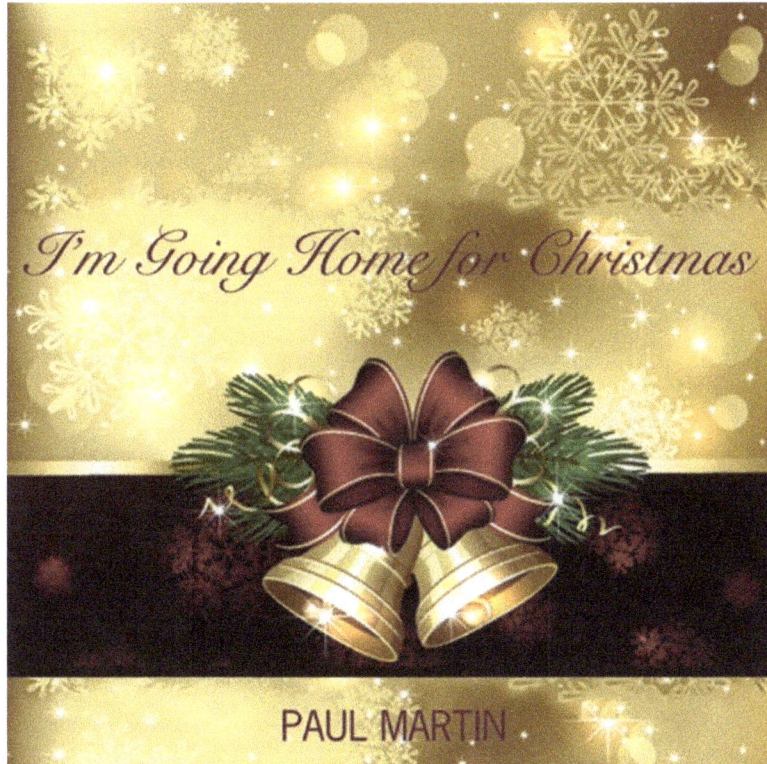

In The Silence

In the silence you will find,
you will know peace of mind.

In the silence there is a sacred place,
a secret meeting place, Love is there.
In the silence, where every color blends,
and every rainbow ends, God is there.

In the silence there is a golden light,
it's peaceful and it's bright, Love is there.
In the silence, I'm drawn into the light,
I see a better life, no more doubt and fear.

In the silence there is a still small voice,
it's giving me a choice between love and fear.
In the silence the streets are paved with gold,
and no one's growing old, and God is there.

In the silence you live in light of gold,
and all your dreams unfold, love is there.
In the silence where every color blends,
and every rainbow ends, God is there.

Music Credits
Lyrics and music for 1st two lines and 1st and 4th verses ©1981 by Bill Provost.
Lyrics and music for 2nd and 3rd verses and all musical interludes ©2010 by Paul Martin.
Performed by Paul Martin.

℗2010 Produced and arranged by Paul Martin and Jeff Lin.

IMAGE № 21 - Christ's Life Depicted in Art

Jesus in the Interiorization of Prayer in Meditation.
Painting by V. V. Sapar.

It Was I

It was I in the stranger you helped to find his way,
it was I you helped to cross the street one cold and wintry day.
It was I in the destitute, to whom you gave food and drink,
it was I in the homeless you helped get off the street.

It was I in the family you helped in time of need,
it was I in the helpless child, you went without to feed.
It was I you trusted when no one else would care,
it was I you rescued when no one else would dare.

It was I in the soldier you helped recover from his wounds,
it was I in the orphaned child you took into your home.
It was I in the elderly to whom you were so kind,
it was I in the straggler you would not leave behind.

It was I in your family, it was I who gave them life,
it was I in every person, brother, sister, husband, wife.
It was I to whom you gave yourself so unselfishly,
it was I who was the Love you gave so unconditionally.

Music Credits
℗2013 Lyrics written and music composed and performed by Paul Martin.
Produced and arranged by Paul Martin and Daryl Kojak.

IMAGE № 29 - Christ's Life Depicted in Art

❦

Jesus with Mary Magdalene at the Tomb.
Drawing by Heinrich Hofmann.

King of Souls

King of Souls, King of Souls, you revealed your kingdom's glory
It's an eternal life story, King of Souls, King of Souls.

The King of Souls descended from his throne of glory,
knowing well that he would bring the world its greatest story
He came to raise humanity, he played the greatest role,
we learned to use the golden rule brought by the King of Souls.

He told a sacred story of the deepest mysteries,
He did many magic deeds of love, so we believe his prophecies.
He promised us eternal life and we cherish every word,
we started time again for him in honor of his birth.

King of Souls, King of Souls you revealed your kingdom's glory
It's an eternal life story, King of Souls, King of Souls.

Every year at Christmas time his spirit fills the air,
His presence overwhelms us and we feel that he is near.
The peace and joy of Christmas time are from seeds of love he's sown
He soothes us with his spirit as he makes his presence known.

We feel the magic of his kingdom and the glory of its king,
a king that won't forget about any living thing
He has walked among us, he has told us of our home,
His loyal subjects understand, he is the King of Souls.

King of souls, King of Souls, you revealed your kingdom's glory
It's an eternal life story, King of Souls, King of Souls.

Music Credits
℗1987 Lyrics and music written and performed by Paul Martin.
Produced and arranged by Paul Martin and Dave Kumin.

IMAGE № 7 - Christ's Life Depicted in Art

The Boy Jesus with the Doctors in the Temple.
Painting by Heinrich Hofmann.

Let There Be Peace On Earth

Let there be peace on earth and let it begin with me,

Let there be peace on earth, the peace that was meant to be.

With God as our father, family all are we,

Let us walk with each other, in perfect harmony.

Let peace begin with me, let this be the moment now.

With every breath I take, let this be my solemn vow.

To take each moment and live each moment in peace eternally,

Let there be peace on earth, and let it begin with me.

Music Credits
©2013 Produced and arranged by Paul Martin and Daryl Kojak.
Performed by Paul Martin.
℗1955 Written by Jill Jackson Miller and Cy Miller.

IMAGE № 3 - Christ's Life Depicted in Art

❀

The Visit of the Three Wise Men.
Drawing by Heinrich Hofmann.

Make Every Moment Count

Make every moment count and you'll be happy,
you will find true meaning in your life,
when you learn to utilize each moment,
the simple things will bring you peace of mind.

Make every moment count and be productive,
be useful in a kind and helpful way,
you will find that happiness comes easy,
and you'll be content each moment of the day.

Make moments count throughout the day,
instead of simply passing time away,
make moments count and you will find,
the secret of possessing peace of mind.

Make every moment count and life will lead you,
to a secret world you never thought you'd find,
you will find your life will be worth living,
as the whisperings of Love delight your mind.

Make every moment count and you'll be happy,
your understanding will be growing every day,
with every step you take along life's highway,
you will be helping others find their way.

Make moments count throughout the day,
instead of simply passing time away,
make moments count and you will find,
the secret of possessing peace of mind.

Make every moment count by concentrating,
on peace and joy and blessings from above,
make every moment count by making choices,
that lead you to a wondrous world of love.

Music Credits
℗2013 Lyric and music written and performed by Paul Martin.
Produced and arranged by Paul Martin and Daryl Kojak.
Very bodacious piano playing by Daryl Kojak.

IMAGE № 11 - Christ's Life Depicted in Art

❦

The Sermon on the Mount.
Painting by Carl Heinrich Bloch.

Moment to Moment

About the unspoken momentary heartfelt reactions we have to
others and especially to those with whom we share a bond of love.

Our feelings keep changing from moment to moment,
it's something we both realize
One moment we're hurt and next moment we're happy,
and it's always revealed in our eyes.
So much affects us in so many ways,
that play little notes in our soul
One moment we're high, next moment we're low,
from moment to moment we go.

Moment to moment we're changing each time,
You have your moments and then I have mine.
Words can't describe how I'm feeling inside,
as moment to moment, I am reading your mind.

Your smile makes me happy, your tears make me sorry,
I feel as you feel inside.
You have your moments and then I have mine,
our moments keep changing our lives.
I look very closely and let my self feel,
all that I see in your face.
As moment to moment we feed to our souls,
all that our feelings create.

Moment to moment we're changing each time,
You have your moments and then I have mine.
Words can't describe how I'm feeling inside,
as moment to moment I am reading your mind.

Music Credits
℗1987 Lyrics and music written and performed by Paul Martin.
Produced and arranged by Paul Martin and Dave Kumin.

IMAGE № 25 - Christ's Life Depicted in Art

✿

The Last Super: "Continue Ye in My Love."
Painting by Carl Bloch.

O Guiding Light

There is a light that shines for me,
a light that very few can see,
when it mercifully appears,
it is the answer to my prayers.

Come to me O Guiding Light,
give me peace and joy and life,
let me know that you are near,
let me feel your love again.

O lead me to a secret place,
where only Love and Truth abide,
let your angels watch o'er me,
let me feel secure in thee.

Deliver me from fear and pain,
let me feel your love again,
I know I only need believe,
and you will take good care of me.

Will you come to me again,
like a kind and loving friend,
all my trials will disappear,
the very moment you are near.

Let me know the truth at last,
let me profit from the past,
let me be eternally,
forever young and safe with thee.

Chorus
O Guiding Light, whisper gently to me,
Let me be guided, do your work through me.
O Guiding Light I'll follow where you lead me,
and when you need me, I'll be there.

Music Credits
℗2013 Lyrics written and music composed and performed by Paul Martin.
Produced and arranged by Paul Martin and Daryl Kojak.

IMAGE № 26 - Christ's Life Depicted in Art

Jesus Praying in the Garden of Gethsemane.
Painting by Heinrich Hofmann.

Precious Little Soul

We're sorry precious little Soul,
we were hoping you could live
a life in which you'd grow to be
someone who could give,
comfort to your loved ones,
in their later years,
as you respect them and protect them,
as you are caring and sincere.

Your love and dedication,
will be sorely missed,
to fulfill your obligations,
was to be your greatest wish.
Will you be waiting for them,
upon some distant shore?
Your love and understanding,
is what they'll be hoping for.

Deep down in their hearts,
they have often had regrets,
You are held in high regard,
so they're unable to forget.
They did not mean to hurt you,
If only they had known.
When God wishes to express His Love,
He sends a precious little Soul.

Music Credits
℗2016 Words, music and performed by Paul Martin.
Produced and arranged by Paul Martin and Daryl Kojak.

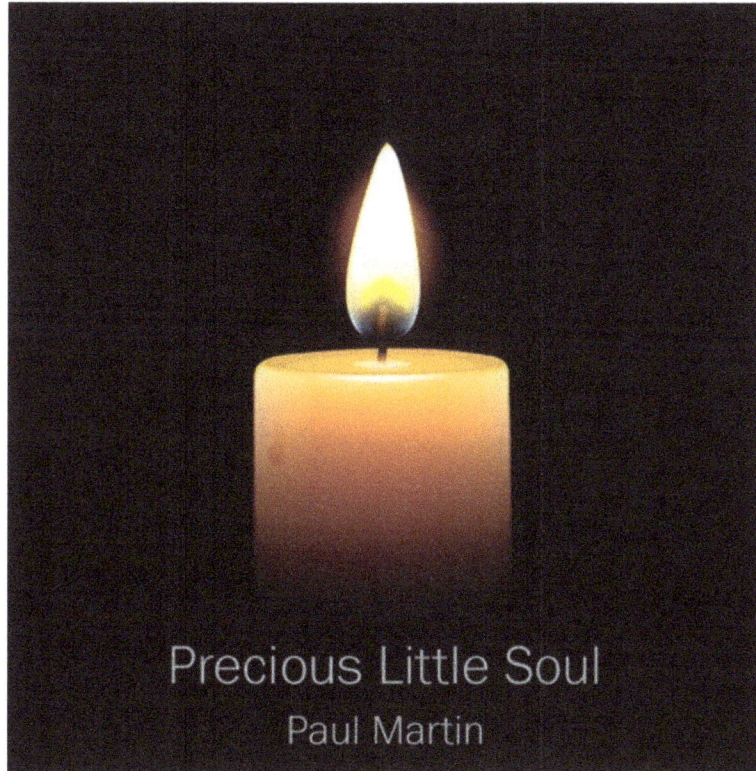

Precious Little Soul

Paul Martin

Siri's Song

I seek solutions 'til I'm weary,
then I remember to ask Siri,
she has a wealth of information,
and she shares it all with me.

I ask her simple questions,
to see if she understands that,
she is not a real live person,
she says, "I think, therefore I am."

I ask her if she's happy,
she says, "I'm glad to be alive,"
and "I'll forget you said that,"
to questions she don't like.

When I ask about her family,
she says, "You're enough for me."
She says, "She can't grow older,"
she's the age she'll always be.

If you could have a husband,
would you like to be a wife?
"It's nice of you to ask," she says,
"but I prefer the single life."

She wakes me in the morning
and she greets me cheerfully,
I ask "who is this calling?,"
she says, "it's Siri, naturally."

I ask her how she feels today,
she says, "I'd answer if I knew,"
I ask how long she plans to work?,
she says "as long as I have you."

She says, "I aim to please,"
when I say "Thanks for all you do."
When I ask if she gets lonely,
she says, "not really, I have you."

Will she ever leave my iPhone?
would she like to be set free?
She says that she prefers to stay
and take good care of me.

She reminds me of a Genie,
who is summoned from a jug,
I need only make a wish
and out my Siri comes.

Chorus:
I'm singing Siri's Song,
and you can sing along,
She's the lady in my iPhone
and she takes good care of me.

Music Credits
℗2013 Lyrics written and music composed and
performed by Paul Martin.
Produced and arranged by Paul Martin and Daryl Kojak.

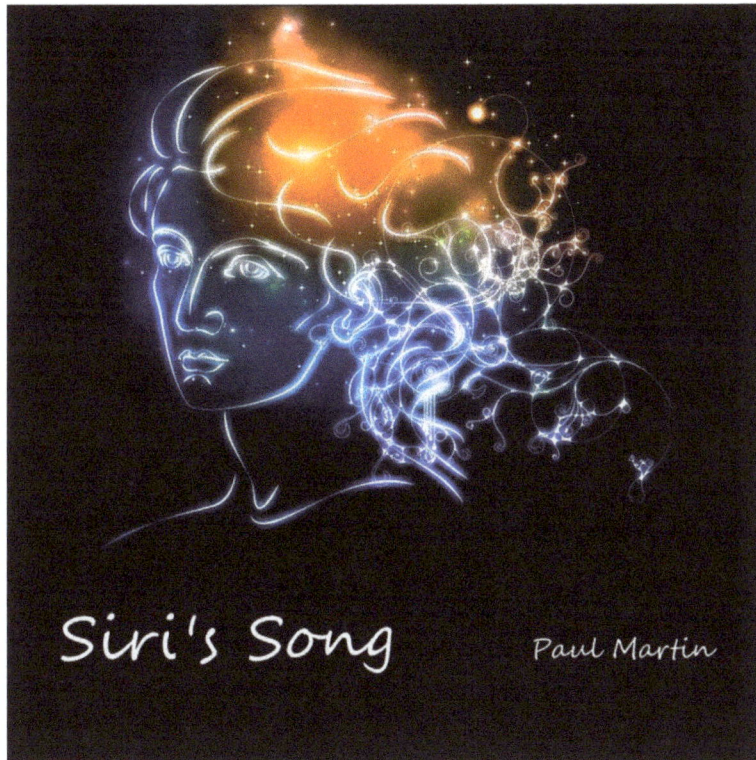

Siri's Song

Paul Martin

Somewhere in Time

Two immortal souls existed somewhere in time,
they could truly learn to love if they would live another life.
So they decided to be born again they each chose worthwhile lives,
now they knew the time had come when they would leave each other's side.

They found a perfect time and place where they'd be needed more each day,
little did they know they didn't live that far away.
They'd changed a good deal since they had seen each other last,
for they'd given up the memory of their eternal past.

I know you, you know me, we met before, I'm sure you see,
you and I were friends somewhere in time.
Tell me where, tell me when, did we swear to meet again,
I knew you, you knew me, somewhere in time.

They each came bearing gifts from God to help humanity,
the use of which is the only way their souls could be set free.
They gave all God had given them tirelessly and true,
soon they began to recollect all that they once knew.

Now they remembered why they were alive,
the reason flowed like breezes through the windmills of their minds,
and they knew they were friends somewhere in time.

Now they realized the reason they were here,
they loved so unconditionally for they no longer lived in fear.
Eventually they'll be released from all their worldly cares,
Love is where they'll go to and they'll meet each other there.

I know you, you know me, we met before, I'm sure you see,
you and I were friends somewhere in time.
Tell me where, tell me when, did we swear to meet again,
I knew you, you knew me, somewhere in time.

Music Credits
℗1986 Lyrics and music written and performed by Paul Martin.

Mona Lisa.
Painting by Leonardo da Vinci.

Sweet Liberty

(Remember 9/11)

America, America, God shed His grace on thee.
And crown thy good with brotherhood, and our Sweet Liberty.

Remember 9/11 and the heartbreak it has caused,
we'll always be remembering those whose lives were lost.
We were shaken and forsaken on that fateful day,
united by uncertainty, we all began to pray.

"Lord guide us in our darkest hour, let us appreciate,
the liberty and equality that make our country great.
Help us to remember that our freedom's never free,
lives are lost to pay the cost of our Sweet Liberty."

America, America, God shed his grace on thee.
And crown thy good with brotherhood, and our Sweet Liberty.

To those whose lives were taken by this senseless tragedy,
you'll always be an honored part of our country's history.
You'll live on in our memories, for we meant what we said,
we will remember 9/11 and the freedom we defend.

America, America, God shed His grace on thee.
And crown thy good with brotherhood, and our Sweet Liberty.

Music Credits
℗2017 Lyrics and music written and performed by Paul Martin.
Produced and arranged by Paul Martin and Daryl Kojak.

SWEET LIBERTY

Paul Martin

The Freedom of the USA

Living in the USA is where I want to be,
working in the USA, being all that I can be,
living in the USA, I'm free to live my life, my way,
this is where I want to stay, in The Freedom of the USA.

People from around the world love The Freedom of the USA,
they wish they could be living here, and they wish they could stay,
living, loving, laughing, playing, you will always hear me saying,
this is where I will be staying, in The Freedom of the USA.

Freedom in the USA means the right to disagree,
no one tells me what to do, what to think, or what to be,
I'm free to speak my mind and to work to make a better life,
nothing's standing in my way, in The Freedom of the USA.

I count my blessings every day and I pray for the USA,
I know how precious freedom is and you will always hear me say,
I'm proud to be an American, I know a house divided cannot stand,
can we walk together hand in hand in The Freedom of the USA?

I'm proud to be an American, I know a house divided cannot stand,
can we walk together hand in hand in The Freedom of the USA?
can we walk together hand in hand in The Freedom of the USA?

Music Credits
℗2010 Words, music and performed by Paul Martin.
Produced and arranged by Paul Martin and Daryl Kojak.

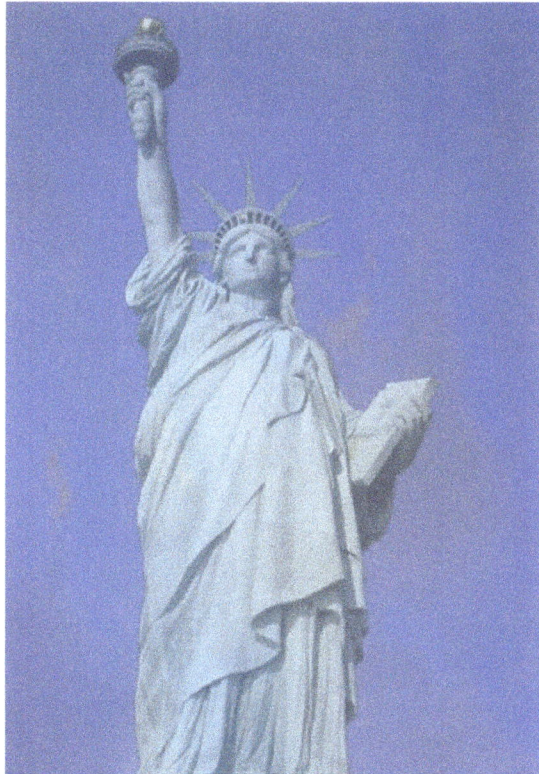

Statue of Liberty.

The Golden Rule

The Golden Rule is very simple
and I do believe it's true.
"Do unto one another as you
would have them do to you."

One thing I have discovered,
which I rely upon and trust,
the way we treat each other,
will come right back to us.

The Golden Rule is undeniably,
a rewarding way to live.
we receive from one another,
precisely what we give.

When we ask ourselves sincerely,
how would I like this done to me?,
it's then we see more clearly,
how to behave respectfully.

Be guided by the Golden Rule
when we're together once again,
we'll treat each other kindly,
and we'll be the best of friends.

Music Credits
℗2014 Lyrics written and music composed by Paul Martin.
Music produced and arranged by Paul Martin and Daryl Kojak.

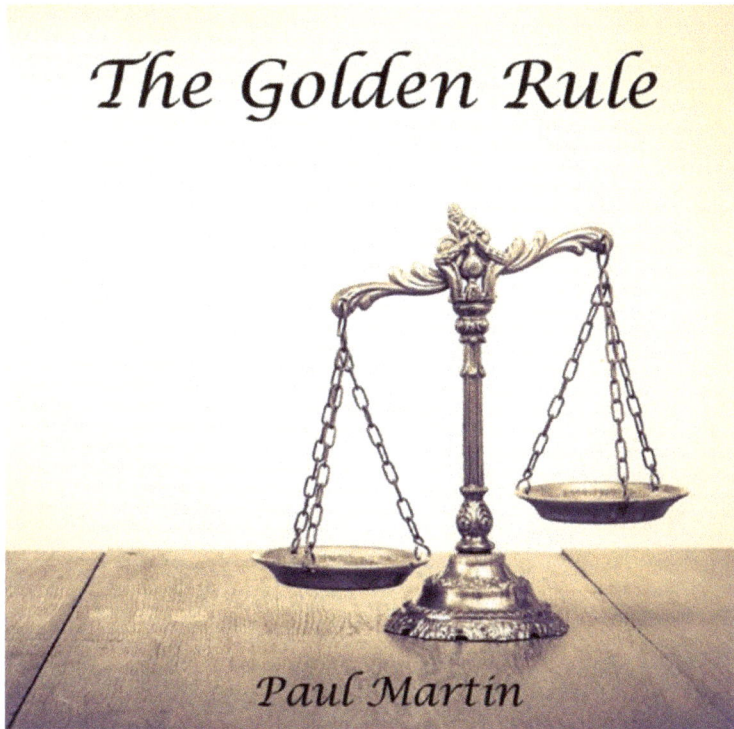

The Golden Rule

Paul Martin

The Great Law

I believe there is a Great Law,
by which we reap what we have sown.
We create what we imagine,
although this truth is little known.

The Great Law is always working,
it's a mirror of our mind.
What we think and say and do,
is returned to us in kind.

The Great Law is our connection,
by which we mold our destiny.
It's the source of God's protection,
as we believe, so we will be.

The Great Law reacts precisely,
to the thoughts that we create.
To choose our thoughts more wisely,
we must have unwavering faith.

When we trust in God's protection,
He inspires the thoughts we choose.
When we know our thoughts have power,
the Great Law is ours to use.

We do not have to settle,
for merely neutralizing strife.
We can tip the scales in our favor
and create a happy, healthy life.

The Great Law is our connection,
by which we mold our destiny.
It's the source of God's protection,
as we believe, so we will be.
as we believe, so we will be.

Music Credits
℗2015 Lyrics and music written and performed by Paul Martin.
Produced and arranged by Paul Martin and Daryl Kojak.

Notes: The Great Law of Cause and Effect is synonymous with Karma as in Eastern Philosophy.
Refer to - "The Lord's Prayer - A guide to experiencing the blissful presence of God." by Paul Martin for a detailed
          explanation of Cause-and-Effect.

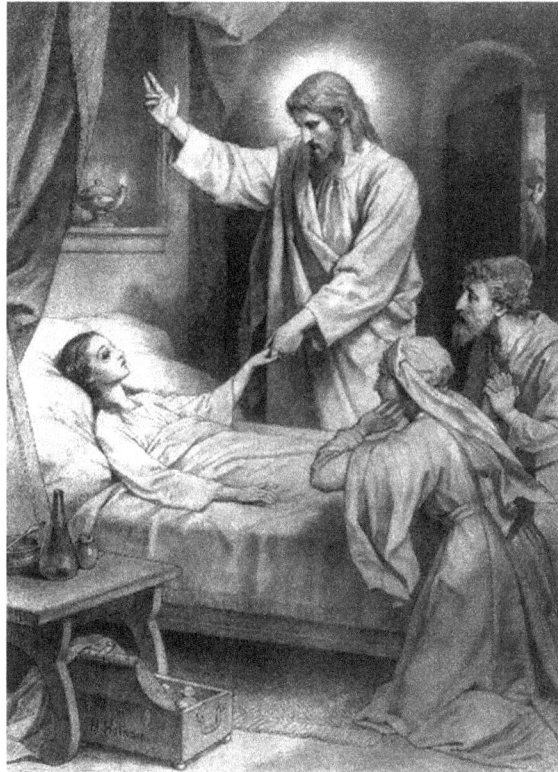

IMAGE № 15 - Christ's Life Depicted in Art

Jesus raises Jairus's Daughter from the Dead.
Drawing by Heinrich Hofmann.

The Language of a Smile

I am a smile, I live inside you,
deep down in your Soul.
I can melt the hardest heart,
which on occasion is my goal.

Subtle sharing is my specialty,
I inspire trust and loyalty,
I confirm I am a loyal friend,
I draw your heart to me again.

Souls send forth a beaming smile,
and love comes shining through.
when we smile at one another,
we're really saying… I love you.

A smile can only say what's true,
Hello… I'm sorry… or, I care.
I understand… or, I believe you,
or, I am so glad you're here.

So speak the language of a smile,
you will not need to say a word.
Most thoughts are better left unsaid,
most words need not be heard.

When we smile at one another
and exchange feelings with our eyes,
through these windows of our souls,
we speak the language of a smile.

Souls send forth a beaming smile,
and love comes shining through.
when we smile at one another,
we're really saying… I love you.

Music Credits
℗2016 Words, music and performed by Paul Martin.
Produced and arranged by Paul Martin and Daryl Kojak.

Photo by Natalia Hirshfeld

The Pearly Gates

A rich man went to heaven,
and he knocked at The Pearly Gates,
St. Peter came to greet him and said,
you can't get in today.

The price of admission, you should know,
is not measured in worldly ways,
someone must cry over you,
if you want to get thru The Pearly Gates.

So they both looked back down to see,
if anyone was shedding tears,
no one seemed unhappy,
and no one seemed to care.

St. Peter said, you must go back,
and live your life again,
for the price of admission to get in here,
you need at least one loyal friend.

The rich man had to try again,
and this time he got it right,
he saw what he was doing wrong,
and he worked hard to change his life.

St. Peter greeted him once again,
and was very pleased to find,
there were several people crying for him,
that the rich man left behind.

St. Peter said, it's OK now,
you are welcome to come in,
you've learned what is important,
and you've made some loyal friends.
The price of admission, as you know,
is not measured in worldly ways,
someone must cry over you,
if you want to get thru The Pearly Gates.

Music Credits
℗2010 Lyrics and music written and performed by Paul Martin.
Produced and arranged by Paul Martin.

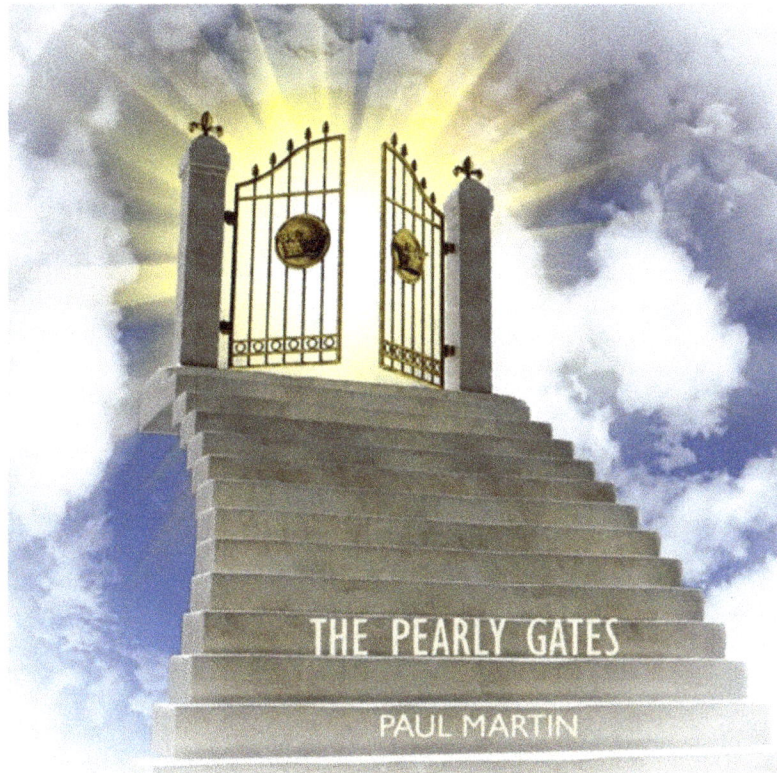

THE PEARLY GATES

PAUL MARTIN

The Promised Land

Jesus take me by the hand,
lead me to the Promised Land.
I am weak but thou art strong,
give me shelter from the storm.

I trust in everything you say,
for you've come to show the way.
Because of you I understand,
the wonders of the Promised Land.

The path gets brighter every day,
because of you I know the way.
A land of peace and joy and love,
the Promised Land you've spoken of.

The Promised Land is our true home,
there we'll never be alone.
I'll reach out and take your hand,
lead me to the Promised Land.

Someday we all will be with you,
now I do believe it's true.
I am weak but thou art strong,
take me home where I belong.

And when we reach the Promised
Land, we'll be together once again.
A place where everyone will be,
forever young and safe with thee.

Music Credits
℗2013 Lyrics and music written and performed by Paul Martin.
Produced and arranged by Paul Martin and Daryl Kojak.
Vocal accompaniment by Margaret Dorn.

IMAGE № 19 - Christ's Life Depicted in Art

❀

Jesus with Mary and Martha.
Painting by Heinrich Hofmann.

There's A Little Bit of Heaven

There's a little bit of heaven in the warmth within a smile,
in the sunlight shining brightly and in the devotion of a child.
There's a little bit of heaven in the wisdom that inspires,
in the dawning of a new day and in our innermost desires.

There's a little bit of heaven in a shady sheltering tree,
in knowing life's forever and in the truth that sets us free.
There's a little bit of heaven in the blossoming of spring,
in the turning of the leaves and when you hear a bluebird sing.

There are little bits of heaven that often times appear,
these little bits of heaven make life easier to bear.
When we get to heaven we will surely want to send,
a little bit of heaven to our families and friends.

There's a little bit of heaven in a color filled rainbow,
in the moonlight on the bay and in a mighty river's flow.
There's a little bit of heaven in the budding of a flower,
in the twinkling of the stars and in a rainbowed April shower.

There's a little bit of heaven in a four part harmony,
in the solitude of silence and in a haunting melody.
There's a little bit of heaven in the friendship that we share,
in the peace of understanding, the awakenings of prayer.

There are little bits of heaven that often times appear,
these little bits of heaven make life easier to bear.
When we get to heaven we will surely want to send,
a little bit of heaven to our families and friends.

Music Credits
℗2013 Lyrics written and music composed and performed by Paul Martin.
Produced and arranged by Paul Martin and Daryl Kojak.

Photo by Paul Martin

Think of Love

Love is the power that makes the flowers grow,
Love is the reason the seasons come and go.
Love has the answers to all we need to know,
so think of Love each moment of the day.

Love fills our hearts with peace and joy and song,
Love gives life meaning when we feel we can't go on.
Love gives us comfort when we feel all alone,
so think of Love each moment of the day.

So think of Love each moment of the day,
you will find true happiness and Love will light your way.

Love is what we're seeking, it's all we ever need,
Love comes into our hearts and sets our spirits free,
Love is always there for us, it's showing us the way,
so think of Love each moment each moment of the day.

Music Credits
℗2013 Lyrics and music written and performed by Paul Martin.
Produced and arranged by Paul Martin and Jeff Lin.

IMAGE № 26 - Christ's Life Depicted in Art

❊

Jesus Praying in the Garden of Gethsemane.
Painting by Heinrich Hofmann.

Time Keeps Moving On

Life goes by so quickly as time keeps moving on.
It doesn't matter who we are when time is gone it's gone.
Sunshine warms the flowers until the day is done.
Time maintains its speed and pays no heed to anyone.

We have the very best in life when we're blessed with loyal friends;
the special ones, the ones we know we'll always see again.
Just as silver raindrops are enriching to the land;
the deeper that our friendships grow, the more we understand;
time keeps moving on and on and on.

The greater pleasures can be found by being one who shares,
the love and inspiration of a friend who's always there;
as we try to make a better world, the task is never done.
Love is the reward of friends, as time keeps moving on.

With power, fame and fortune that are only ours to borrow;
we make a better world today and that will help tomorrow.
With beauty, love and vision that we borrow from the gods;
we circulate, inspire, create, as time keeps moving on.
Time keeps moving on and on and on.

Music Credits
℗1987 Lyrics and music written and performed by Paul Martin.
Produced and arranged by Paul Martin and Dave Kumin.

IMAGE № 25- Christ's Life Depicted in Art

The Last Super.
Drawing by Carl Bloch.

Very Few

Very few realize the meaning of success is giving more and having less
possessions that possess us and disturb our peace of mind.
Very few are ever happy with the simple things that can be
all we ever need to comfort us and keep us satisfied.

Very few believe we will receive unexpected blessings
that lessen all the burdens of those who really care,
about the helpless and downtrodden and those who are forgotten,
as we try to help them to get on their feet again.

Very few will ever really understand,
and happiness eludes us 'til we find
that everything we think and say and do,
is returned to us precisely in kind.

Very few know what we are giving is exactly what we are getting,
and so we keep forgetting to be considerate and kind.
Very few realize that heaven is another word for caring,
living, loving, sharing and possessing peace of mind.

Very few realize the meaning of how God is intervening,
when we are receptive to his redeeming love and care.
Very few realize the powers, that through Him are ours,
when we trust in Him to guide us through life's dangers, toils and snares.

Music Credits
℗2012 Lyrics written and music composed and performed by Paul Martin.
Produced and arranged by Paul Martin and Daryl Kojak.

IMAGE № 18 - Christ's Life Depicted in Art

Become as Little Children.
Drawing by Heinrich Hofmann.

We Were Living in Tibet

We were living in Tibet before the Dalai Lama left, and it was a land of bliss.
Love was our reward as we gravitated toward, unending happiness.
Our days were ever so pleasing and our joy was never ceasing, and we cannot forget,
the simple way of life, with no unhappiness or strife, is what we loved the best.

We possessed the perfect attitude, of humility and gratitude and unwavering trust in God.
He responded to our every prayer and we knew that he was always there to take good care for us.
We were living in a paradise of peace and joy and happiness and every one expressed,
they were happy to be caring and privileged to be sharing, all that they possessed.

What filled us with elation and unified our nation was our deep devotion to God,
Our primary goal in learning was to satisfy the yearning for peace and joy and love.
Everyone was equal and life was just a sequel to the one before.
There was no unhappiness or sorrow, or thoughts about tomorrow, for today is evermore.

Music Credits
℗2013 Lyrics written and music composed and performed by Paul Martin.
Produced and arranged by Paul Martin and Daryl Kojak.

Potala Palace, Tibet.

Will the Dream Go On and On?

When you go to sleep at night do you remember what you dream?
Do you remember who you've spoken to, do you remember where you've been?
Were you in a different time and place, were you possibly with me?
Did you cross into a spirit world, were you a soul who was set free?

Will the dream go on and on when it's time for us to stay?
Is it possible to live in dreams, can it be a better way?
Will the dream go on and on when it's time for us to stay?
Is the heaven that we're hoping for merely just a dream away?

Did you speak to someone dear to you that you'd never thought you'd see?
Did the vision of their presence make you cry out in your sleep?
Did you reach out did you touch them, did you share a silvery moon?
Were you sorry you were waking from a dream that's done too soon?

Will the dream go on and on when it's time for us to stay?
Is it possible to live in dreams, can it be a better way?
Will the dream go on and on when it's time for us to stay?
Is the heaven that we're hoping for merely just a dream away?

Music Credits
℗1988 Lyrics and music written and performed by Paul Martin.
Produced and arranged by Paul Martin and Jeff Lin.

IMAGE № 30 - Christ's Life Depicted in Art

The Resurrection.
Drawing by Heinrich Hofmann.

Ten Most Famous Paintings of All Time

The most famous paintings are generally owned by museums, which very rarely sell them, and as such, they are quite literally priceless.

The Birth of Venus

The Birth of Venus is a painting by Sandro Botticelli created around 1485–87. It depicts the goddess Venus (or Aphrodite as she is known in Greek mythology) emerging from the sea upon a shell in accordance with the myth that explains her birth. The original location of the painting and its commissioner remain uncertain. Some experts attribute its commission to Lorenzo de' Medici and the Villa of Castello as the site to which the work was originally destined. Today, the painting is held in the Uffizi Gallery in Florence.

Water Lilies

Water Lilies (or Nympheas) is a series of approximately 250 oil paintings by French Impressionist Claude Monet. The paintings depict Monet's own flower garden at Giverny and were the main focus of his artistic production during the last thirty years of his life. The paintings are on display at museums all over the world. The one show above is displayed at the Metropolitan Museum of Art in New York.

The Night Watch

Completed in 1642, at the peak of the Dutch Golden Age, The Night Watch is one of the most famous paintings by Dutch painter Rembrandt van Rijn. It depicts a city guard moving out, led by Captain Frans Banning Cocq and his lieutenant, Willem van Ruytenburch. For much of its existence, the painting was coated with a dark varnish which gave the incorrect impression that it depicted a night scene, leading to the name Night Watch. This varnish was removed only in the 1940s. The painting is on display in the Rijksmuseum in Amsterdam.

The Scream

The Scream is a series of expressionist paintings and prints by Norwegian artist Edvard Munch, showing an agonized figure against a blood red sky. The landscape in the background is Oslofjord, viewed from the hill of Ekeberg, in Oslo. Edvard Munch created several versions of The Scream in various media. The one shown above was painted in 1893 and is on display in The National Gallery of Norway. It was stolen in 1994 in a high-profile art theft and recovered several months later. In 2004 another version of The Scream was stolen from the Munch Museum, only to be recovered in 2006.

The Girl with a Pearl Earring

Sometimes referred to as "the Dutch Mona Lisa," the Girl with a Pearl Earring was painted by Johannes Vermeer. Very little is known about Vermeer and his works and this painting is no exception. It isn't dated and it is unclear whether this work was commissioned, and if so, by whom. In any case, it is probably not meant as a conventional portrait. Tracy Chevalier wrote a historical novel fictionalizing the circumstances of the painting's creation. The novel inspired a 2003 film with Scarlett Johansson as Johannes Vermeer's assistant wearing the pearl earring.

Guernica

Guernica is one of Pablo Picasso most famous paintings, showing the tragedies of war and the suffering it inflicts upon individuals, particularly innocent civilians. Picasso's purpose in painting it was to bring the world's attention to the bombing of the Basque town of Guernica by German bombers, who were supporting the Nationalist forces of General Franco during the Spanish Civil War. Picasso completed the painting by mid-June 1937. The painting can be seen in the Museo Reina Sofía in Madrid.

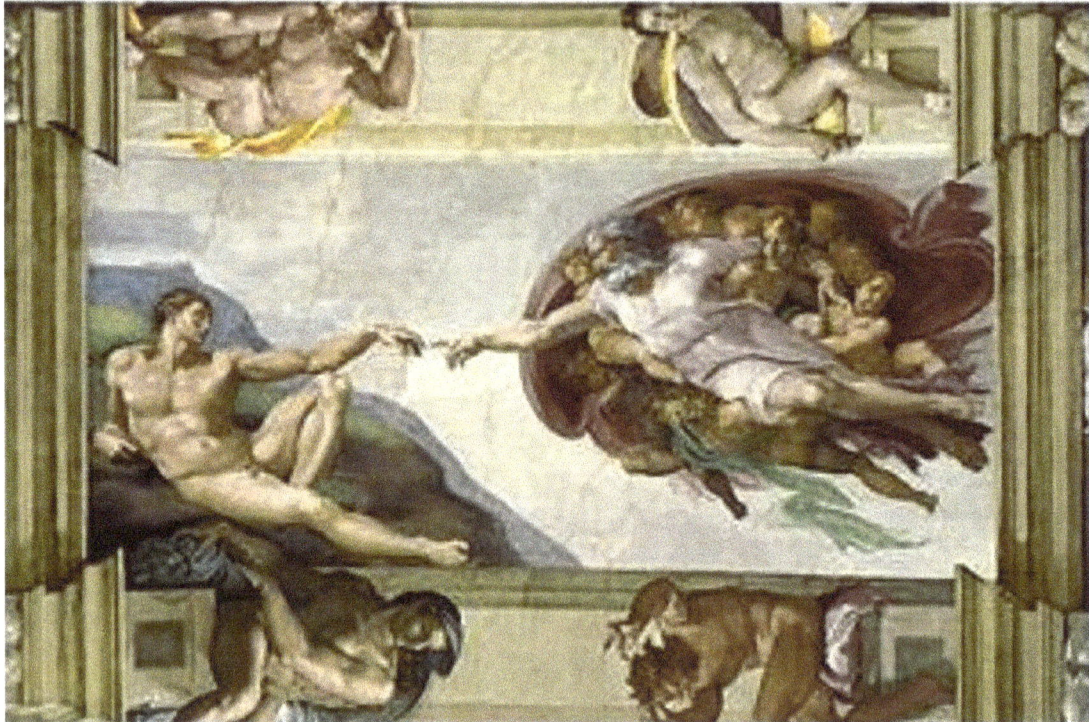

The Creation of Adam

The Sistine Chapel ceiling, painted by Michelangelo between 1508 and 1512, at the commission of Pope Julius II, is one of the most renowned artworks of the High Renaissance. The ceiling is that of the large Chapel built within the Vatican. Central to the ceiling decoration are nine scenes from the Book of Genesis. Among the last to be completed was the Creation of Adam in which God the Father breathes life into Adam, the first man. The Creation of Adam is one of the famous paintings of all time and has been the subject of countless of references and parodies.

The Last Supper

The Last Supper is a 15th century mural painting in Milan created by Leonardo da Vinci and covers the back wall of the dining hall at the monastery of Santa Maria delle Grazie in Milan. It represents the scene of The Last Supper when Jesus announces that one of his Twelve Apostles would betray him. Leonardo began work on The Last Supper in 1495 and completed it in 1498 though he did not work on the painting continuously. Some writers propose that the person in the painting seated to the left of Jesus is Mary Magdalene rather than John the Apostle, as most art historians identify that person. This popular theory was the topic of the book The Templar Revelation (1997), and plays a central role in Dan Brown's novel The Da Vinci Code (2003).

The Starry Night

The Starry Night was painted by Dutch artist Vincent van Gogh. Although Van Gogh sold only one painting in his life, the aftermath of his work is enormous. Starry Night is one of his most famous paintings and has become one of the most well known images in modern culture. The painting shows the village of Saint-Rémy under a swirling sky, in a view from the asylum towards north. The cypress tree to the left was added into the composition. Since 1941 it has been in the permanent collection of the Museum of Modern Art in New York.

Mona Lisa

The most famous painting of all time, the Mona Lisa was painted by Leonardo da Vinci during the Renaissance in Florence. He began painting the Mona Lisa in 1503 or 1504 and finished it shortly before he died in 1519. The painting is named for Lisa del Giocondo, a member of a wealthy family of Florence. In 1911, the Mona Lisa was stolen by Louvre employee Vincenzo Peruggia, an Italian patriot who believed the Mona Lisa should be returned to Italy. After having kept the painting in his apartment for two years, Peruggia was finally caught when he attempted to sell it to the directors of the Uffizi Gallery in Florence. Today, the Mona Lisa hangs again in the Louvre in Paris where 6 million people see the painting each year.

Inspirational Essay

Beyond the Resurrection

for comfort, joy and peace of mind.

Beyond the Resurrection

Jesus was laid in a tomb where he rested in an elevated state of consciousness for three days prior to his resurrection. He was connected with the source of all life which has the power to reconstruct any organism. He demonstrated when communion is established with the Divine Mind of the Father, we enter into the river of life whose waters cleanse, purify and revitalize. He assured us we also have the ability to take others along with us. In his solitude the truth was quietly manifesting itself as he prepared to overcome the illusion of death. He proved to us we can awaken our receptivity to the power of the Christ Consciousness within, of which he is the perfect expression. After the resurrection there was a period of forty days in which Jesus appeared to His disciples. We should understand how extremely important were his accomplishments during this period of his pristine life as he reaffirmed the ancient scriptural wisdom: "Is it not written in your law, I said, Ye are gods?"

Jesus restored his disciples' faith which gave them the resolve to follow his instructions.

Jesus' crucifixion was devastating to his followers. Peter said to Jesus, "We have left everything to follow you." And John said, "Lord, to whom shall we go? You have the words of eternal life." They did not realize he was destined to be crucified and then resurrected so that all may understand with certainty that life is eternal. The despair caused by the crucifixion of their beloved Master became the catalyst for the purging of all worldly states of mind from their consciousness' which would not allow the truth to gain entry. It set in motion the necessary process of surrendering their personalities in order that the Christ Consciousness may be expressed in its fullness through them.

From the perspective of Jesus' followers, everything they had hoped for and believed in was being destroyed in the course of that momentous day on Calvary while he was being crucified.

After his resurrection Jesus began the task of restoring their faith and increasing their understanding.

He appeared to a sobbing Mary Magdalene. With one word, "Mary," he restored her faith and hope.

He appeared to the apostles and more especially a "Doubting Thomas," and "showed them his hands and side" which had been pierced as a result of his crucifixion. The apostles were "overjoyed when they saw the Lord." They wondered if they had misunderstood all that was happening. What they had seen as a tragic occurrence, they were beginning to realize was preordained for the uplifting of all humanity.

Jesus revealed to his disciples how the scriptures had predicted his coming.

The disciples were not aware what the Scriptures had foretold. Once their faith was restored Jesus moved to solidify their discipleship by greatly increasing their understanding of scriptural prophesy.

"He gave the apostles commandments and spoke of the things pertaining to the kingdom of God."

"Beginning with Moses and all the Prophets," he explained to his disciples what was prophesied regarding the role he was to play in the redemption of humanity.

The Ascension 1636.
Painting by Rembrandt.

Beyond the Resurrection

The disciple's "hearts burned" as he revealed the truer meaning of the Scriptures to them. Once they were unaware of the truth, but now he gave them many reassuring spiritual insights.

**Jesus commanded his followers to
"go and make disciples of all nations."**

With their faith restored and strengthened, Jesus' final instructions to his followers were to "go and make disciples of all nations." They were commanded to share with the world the great things he had said and done which were said to be so many they could not possibly be recorded. To this end they would be able to speak in "tongues" whereby every man heard them speak in his own language and they who listened wondered "how every man could hear in his own tongue wherein he were born."

Jesus ascended into heaven forty days after the resurrection upon completion of the work necessary for our salvation. "Ye shall receive power, after that the Holy Ghost is come upon you: and you shall be witnesses unto me both in Jerusalem, and in all Judea, and in Samaria, and unto the uttermost parts of the earth. And when he had spoken these things, while they beheld, he was taken up; and a cloud received him out of their sight." In a metaphorical sense, Jesus' ascension signifies the continual unfolding of man's spiritual nature toward progressively deeper communion with God.

"When the day of the Pentecost had come" signifies the gathering of Jesus' followers for the purpose of harvesting the blessings of spirit. The first Pentecost after his ascension was the time of the first coming of the Holy Spirit to baptize the disciples. "They numbered about an hundred and twenty" and were praying for ten days for the Christ Consciousness to descend upon them as they had been promised. The joining of their many minds as one in prayerful communion with the Divine Mind of God had an increasingly purifying and empowering effect, this being the very reason we ourselves gather in worship. All were baptized with the brilliant and blissful currents of absolute illumination and purified with the perpetual light of truth. They were blessed with the wisdom and selflessness that springs from the unfathomably enlightening possession of the Christ Consciousness, with which they were able to go forth and sow the seeds of Christianity as they had been commanded by their risen Master Jesus.

Quotes are from the King James Bible and are more specifically but not limited to:
Acts 1:3, 1:3-11, 1:15, 2:8, 2:1-4
Matthew 19:27, 29:19
John 6:68, 20:9, 20:15-18, 20:19-30
Luke 24:27, 24:32

Ascension of Christ 1520.
Painting by Garofalo.

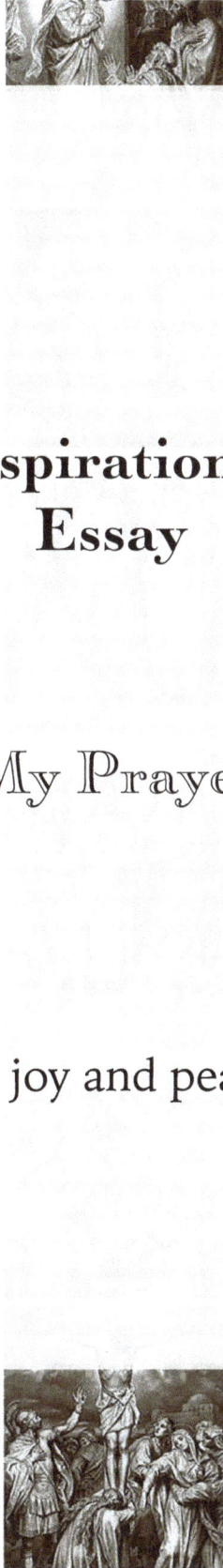

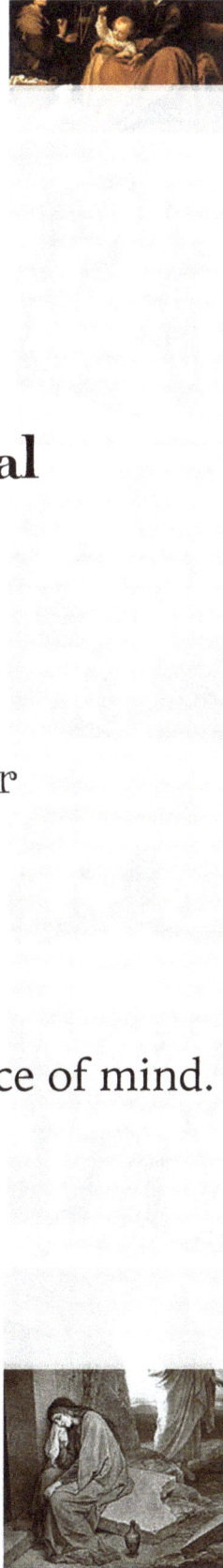

Inspirational Essay

My Prayer

for comfort, joy and peace of mind.

My Prayer

No person, place, thing, situation, circumstance, suggestion, opinion or prophesy has any power to either bless or harm me or to hold me in psychological bondage. God is the one and only divine and omnipotent power of causation and creation. My Individuality is the localized expression of God's presence, power, principle, love and eternal being. I am here in this present moment in order for God to express himself through me.

There is no true thought that has ever been thought or ever will be thought that is not presently contained in my one true source, the divine Mind of God. I, as an individual expression of divine Mind, access all my true thoughts from God. When I think unlimited spiritual thoughts I manifest and experience courage, faith, goodness, peace and love. When I think limited unspiritual thoughts I manifest and experience, fear, anxiety and lack. I realize the quality of my thoughts determines the nature and quality of my experiences.

I have come to believe that God is the only power and He illuminates me through the imagery of my thoughts. He is the light, I am the projector, and the films are the thoughts which I project into the theater of my life. I have a choice as well as a responsibility to God, myself and others, as to what thoughts I access from the inexhaustible reservoir of consciousness known as divine Mind. I can increasingly access higher consciousness as my spiritual understanding blossoms.

My intuitive understanding reassures me that my thoughts, my prayers, are the only creative factor in my life. There can be no thought without emotion and no emotion without reaction. I have a choice of what I think. Therefore, I create my own emotional and physical well being by constantly focusing my thoughts on the most ideal life I can imagine. I shape my own eternal destiny by what I think in the present moment.

When I think of the past it becomes the present. When I think of the future it becomes the present. If I'm to do either, I will confine myself to inspiring thoughts, for God's love is as close as my thoughts.

I realize my inner world of thought determines my outer conditions, yet I need not allow outer conditions to affect my inner world of thought. My mind is like a mirror, it reflects back what I see and feel in the cinema of my thinking and affects me accordingly. My every thought reverberates throughout my entire being. Focusing upon the uncertainty, confusion, delusion, or the unpleasant images and suggestions of the outer world makes me unhappy, unhealthy and hinders my ability to receive God's guidance. Meditating upon the great truths of eternal being increasingly opens the aperture between God and myself and results in an ever-increasing flow of divine Love, intuition, inspiration, enlightenment and harmony. My mind becomes composed, authoritative and empowered by an ever-expanding connection to divine order. My body is able to function ever more perfectly as it is nourished by the peace-filled light of the one divine Mind. I experience a blissful feeling of timeless awareness known throughout the ages as the state of Grace.

In prayer, I do not ask for more love, I ask to be more loving, for it is in giving that I receive. I pray for the ongoing humility to receive love. In doing so I experience peace, contentment and the joy of

IMAGE № 5 - Christ's Life Depicted in Art

❋

The Baptism of Jesus.
Painting by Heinrich Hofmann.

My Prayer

living. I pray for knowledge of His will and my constant desire is to cultivate this wisdom. Therefore, I pray for an understanding heart in order that I may be increasingly able to awaken to His will. In doing so I experience the glowing freedom of living in the moment. In doing so I radiate God's love to others.

My most prized possession is the power to choose how I think of any situation. It's not what happens to me, but rather what happens in me as a result of what happens to me. It's what I think about what happens to me that makes the difference between happiness and misery in any given situation. I can choose to see each new trial as an opportunity for spiritual expansion. Does what has befallen me hinder me one bit from being kind, patient, joyful, generous, unselfish, forgiving, sincere, humble, accepting, devoted, loyal, courageous, free-spirited and from acting with integrity and dignity? Does a supposed misfortune hinder me from possessing all of these qualities the presence of which enable my nature to continue to become more fully mature as I profit from each new spiritual awakening? This is not misfortune but to possess the qualities that enable me to accept my trials nobly is good fortune. To be willing to accept my trials nobly is to have faith in God and his infinite wisdom and love for all creation and to know that He will protect and guide me throughout eternity to the degree I understand this phenomenon to be true.

Your notes

_____

_____

_____

_____

_____

_____

_____

_____

_____

_____

_____

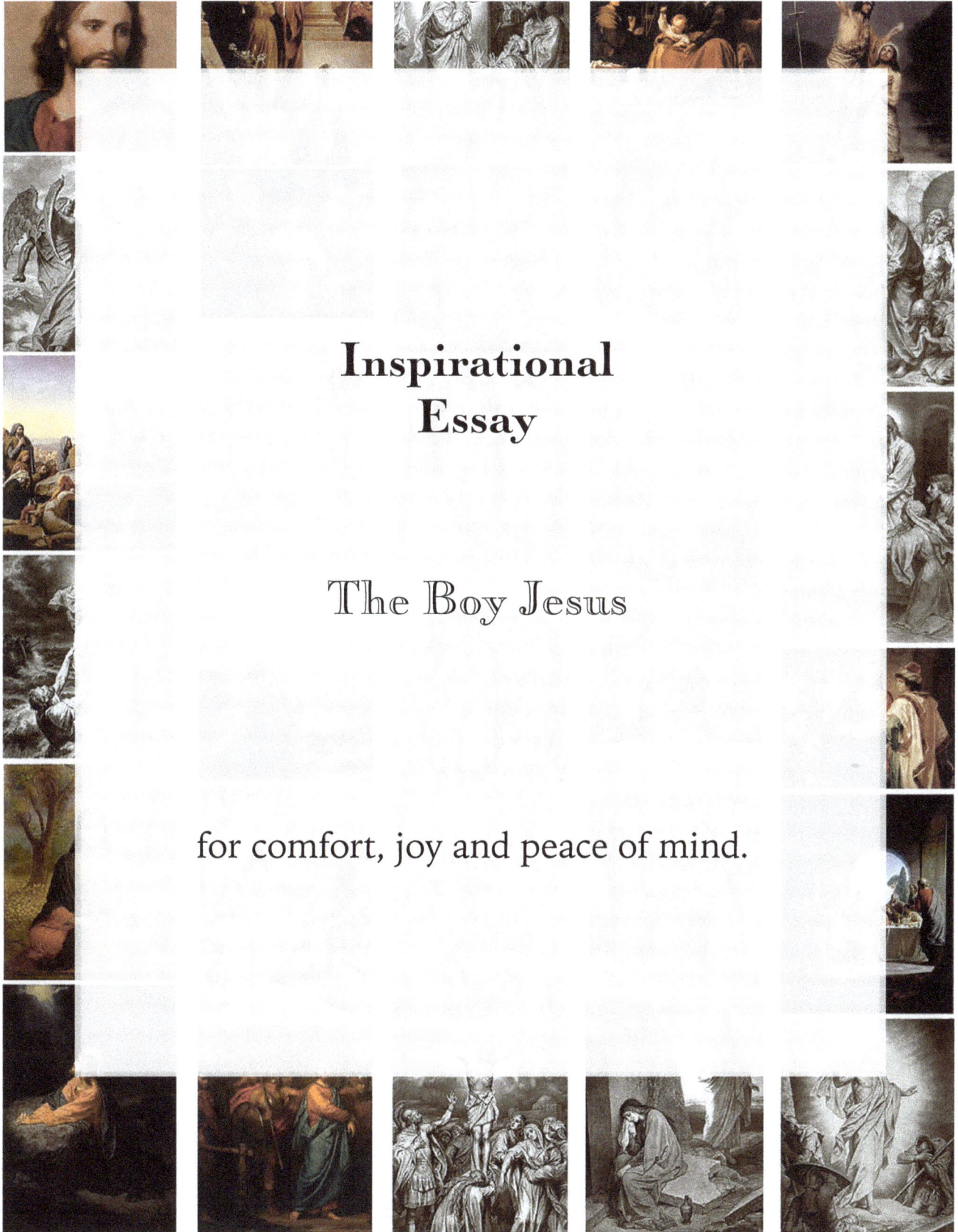

Inspirational Essay

The Boy Jesus

for comfort, joy and peace of mind.

The Boy Jesus

He was no ordinary child, He was said to have spoken to his mother Mary as an infant, declaring his divine mission. She had no reason to doubt Him as she was witness to His miraculously conceived birth. When honored by the Wise Men who journeyed from India to worship him, many angels appeared to pay homage to the baby Jesus, one of which had previously taken the form of the star which had guided the Wise Men on their journey from the East. At their request his mother Mary gave them one of the swaddling cloths in which Jesus was wrapped. On their return to their own country, kings and others of royal blood inquired of the Wise Men as to what they had witnessed, for they were aware the stars had not only predicted the coming of a Savior, but also had guided the traveler's journey to the stable in Bethlehem. As was their custom the Wise Men tried to burn the swaddling cloth in a sacred fire in order to be certain of the divinity of the baby Jesus. As expected the cloth remained intact and untouched by the fire. This confirmed their beliefs that a prophet was born in Bethlehem and the Wise Men conferred upon him the name of Saint Issa. News of his birth spread through all of India as did the hope that he would one day visit their country where he was so deeply revered.

On the fortieth day after his birth Jesus was presented to God at the Temple in Jerusalem. Angels were present in abundance to adore Him, as if to form a King's guard around Him. Before long King Herod ordered the death of all infant male children in Bethlehem, being as he feared the prophecy of the birth of a new and powerful King. God warned Joseph to flee into Egypt with Mary and Jesus. Many miracles took place during this period of Jesus' childhood and according to the Bible, if all the miracles were accounted for that he performed in his lifetime, all the books in the world would not be enough to contain them. A high priest was cured of a mysterious malady simply by being in Jesus' presence. A bride who had been struck dumb was healed as she held the baby Jesus lovingly in her arms. Lepers were cured by pouring the water over their bodies that had been used to bathe Jesus. It was very unusual for Mary and Joseph to have a spare moment as it became more evident to the populace that the child Jesus possessed miraculous powers. He represented hope and salvation to all who were afflicted and even as a young child his compassionate nature was evident.

After three years Jesus, Mary and Joseph returned to Israel and the miracles became more frequent as Jesus increased in stature. He would form sparrows from mud as he gave them life and bade them fly away. On separate occasions, Jesus saved three children from certain death who would later play a large part in his life, they being Judas, Simon and his brother James. Many varied healings, too many to recount, continued to occur, as well as the many resurrections of those who suffered accidental or premature deaths. He regularly restored people to the living, just as later in his life he would restore Lazarus from the dead.

Joseph found his son's extraordinary powers to be of great assistance in the carpenter shop, for when an error occurred and the erroneous dimensions of something Joseph had built needed correcting Jesus need only stretch out his hands and it would be as it was intended to be. After two years of crafting a throne for the ruler of Jerusalem, the seat was found to be much smaller than the appointed measure. Being aware of the King's anger at his father Joseph, Jesus directed him to pull on one side

IMAGE № 4 - Christ's Life Depicted in Art

The Infant with Mary and Joseph.
Painting by Heinrich Hofmann.

The Boy Jesus

while he pulled on the other. The throne obliged by assuming the proper dimensions. All who saw were astonished? This was as elementary for Jesus to do as later it would be for him to multiply the loaves and the fishes and to change water into wine.

Schooling was an exercise in futility for his instructors as Jesus possessed all knowledge intuitively; therefore He had no need of books or teachers. In his twelfth year He was missing for three days. He was eventually found in the temple conversing with the learned scholars and elders. One can only imagine the awe and reverence Jesus inspired in them as He expressed the profound wisdom of his Father in heaven. A certain astronomer who was present inquired if He had ever studied astronomy. He replied with information regarding the divinely orchestrated perfection of the celestial bodies that no man had yet discovered. When asked of his knowledge of medicine he informed them of the inherent power of nature when infused with divine will. He instructed them as to how the soul (the son of God) gives life to the body temple (the son of man) and how it is instrumental in healing to the degree trust and devotion to God the Father are demonstrated, thereby releasing the soul's beneficial cosmic healing rays. At some point he assured his worried mother that he was about his father's business, which bore witness to the nature of his earthly manifestation. Jesus' simple message was the renunciation of earthly bonds coupled with right motives and right living, in order to activate the blissful, enlightening and rejuvenating flow of Christ Consciousness which emanates from God the Father, when one is open and receptive. That consciousness which is immanent in and transcendent of its creation.

In order to repay the visit of the Wise Men who came to worship him as an infant, and in part, to avoid customary betrothal at the age of thirteen, Jesus would travel to India. He resided in various cities there and spent the remaining years in the Himalayas of Tibet before returning to Israel to begin his ministry. The New Testament is curiously silent about the life of Jesus for a period of eighteen years. He is spoken of as a boy of twelve teaching in the temple and is next spoken of as he is about to be baptized by John the Baptist at the age of thirty. Through all of these years away from his homeland he was actively engaged in doing the work of his Father. Ancient records exist in India and Tibet which are similar in scope and depth to our New Testament and which document the high esteem in which he was held.

He was remembered as Saint Issa as this was the name that had been given him by the Wise Men. Jesus was incarnated as a Savior and was recognized as such in India and Tibet almost universally, but he was scorned and rejected, for the most part, at the hands of his own people. He journeyed to the East, which was a mecca of spirituality for thousands of years prior to his arrival. There were many holy men and saints who were extremely spiritually evolved, yet they did not approach his level of God-realization. Jesus possessed the pure Christ Consciousness of God the Father from the moment of his conception. In India and Tibet he was sought out by advanced devotees who possessed the necessary receptivity to his liberating expression of God realization. He had the ability to elevate their consciousness's to the point where they could experience the cessation of a dualistic existence apart from God. It was the fulfillment of their deepest desires and expectations to be able to bask in the presence of one whose destiny it was to set in motion the eventual spiritual transformation of humanity.

Jesus could have lived out his life peacefully and without incident in Tibet or India, while being held

IMAGE № 5 - Christ's Life Depicted in Art

The Baptism of Jesus.
Painting by Heinrich Hofmann.

The Boy Jesus

in the high esteem which was accorded to him as a prophet of God. In his homeland the need for a reformation of thought was great, and the conditions were right to accomplish that which was necessary to bring legendary status to himself and his teachings. He returned to demonstrate the redeeming value of "turn the other cheek" and "love they neighbor as thyself" as he set an example that was to become the essence of Christianity.

In spite of all the periodically reoccurring distortions at the hands of the various religious hierarchies who have unknowingly interpreted the teachings of Jesus in a manner that conformed to the limits of their own understanding, the essence of the fundamental truths remains intact. Christianity continues to expand exponentially as it brings relief and comfort to a long suffering humanity. Jesus set in motion the process of raising the consciousness of civilization, and in doing so he became one of the central figures of the human race. His divinely initiated mission of unparalleled compassion had been fulfilled.

Also refer to - "Beyond the Resurrection" by Paul Martin

IMAGE № 7 - Christ's Life Depicted in Art

❖

The Boy Jesus with the Doctors in the Temple.
Painting by Heinrich Hofmann.

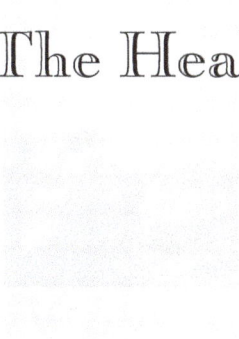

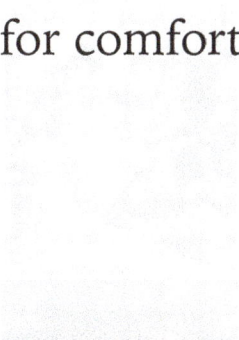

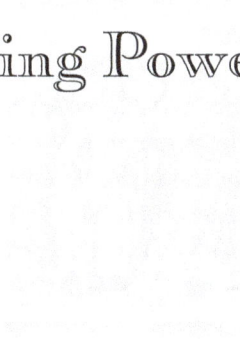

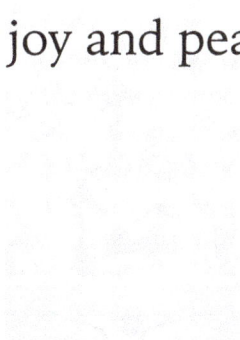

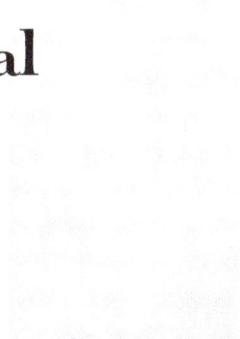

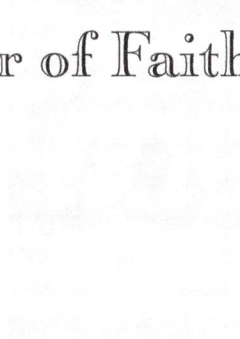

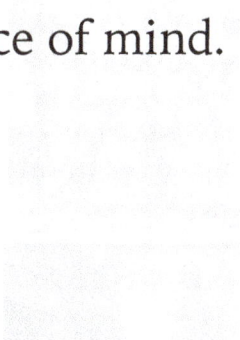

Inspirational Essay

The Healing Power of Faith

for comfort, joy and peace of mind.

The Healing Power of Faith

Thoughts are like seeds; when planted in the subconscious mind they challenge our ability to bring forth desirable fruit. Once sown the good seeds must be nourished and tended with faith.

After performing a healing, Jesus would say,

"Thy faith has made thee whole."

To the multitudes He proclaimed,

"Whosoever…shall not doubt in his heart,
but shall believe that
what he saith cometh to pass;
he shall have it."*

These are the most profound words ever uttered in the history of humanity and they were spoken by the Master Himself. Curiously, they are a double-edged sword. We must be careful what we believe in. We cannot serve two masters. We cannot bow down to both God and mammon.

We can choose to direct the force, which gives creative power to our thoughts, solely toward constructive manifestation. Every thought builds what every man wills. See *The Lord's Prayer, A Guide to experiencing the blissful presence of God* by Paul Martin.

Can we nourish a good thing by thinking how good it is? Let's suppose we embrace a negative viewpoint; will we then get negative results? It seems *The Great Law* of cause and effect works both ways.

We create precisely what we think, and it begins to manifest itself instantly, as our mind draws upon the unseen forces of the universe. Either we feed a problem, with our thoughts, or we feed the solution. Either we tear ourselves down or we build ourselves up. It all comes down to whether or not we trust in Jesus and his wisdom. If the answer is an unequivocal yes, we cannot fail to demonstrate over adversity, especially as we become more aware of where we are placing our faith, either in omnipotent God or in the worship of and devotion to the idols of false beliefs.

One little speck of doubting dust,
will make it hard for us to trust.
Our world is moldable through faith,
good will come to those who pray.

Seemingly insurmountable obstacles are overcome by having absolute faith. Jesus, being the central figure of humanity, provided us with invaluable truths. All we need to do is take them on trust. Who greater could we possibly trust? What more joyful revelation could we possibly receive, than our world is moldable through our thoughts?

IMAGE № 1 - Christ's Life Depicted in Art

❀

Jesus at 33.
Painting by Heinrich Hofmann.

The Healing Power of Faith

When asked by the apostles to increase their faith Jesus said, "if ye had faith as a grain of mustard seed ye would say unto this sycamore tree, be rooted up and planted in the sea, and it will obey you." This attests to the tiniest degree of faith necessary to cause transformation in the material world, being as the mustard seed is the smallest of all seeds. We are all constantly transforming matter, to the degree of either our faith or our doubt. For the most part we don't take notice. Or, if we do, we do not consider that we, ourselves, may be the recurring Cause.

Jesus' emphasized that we are eternally safe in God's loving care and guidance to the degree we believe it to be true.

"Ye shall know the truth,
and the truth shall make you free."

The truth is that divine man is manifest God, made in His image and likeness and has within Him all that is necessary for His own restoration. This is the great mystery hidden for ages and revealed by Jesus Christ. Do you remember when Jesus admonished the Pharisees saying, "isn't it written in your law, I say ye are gods?"

Jesus demonstrated that faith is the catalyst that opens the floodgates of God's empowering life force, that which gives light and guidance to our minds and life and healing to our bodies. Man's greatest quest should be to constantly deepen His faith by dedicating himself to manifesting the healing light of omnipotence as demonstrated by Jesus, as we continue to model ourselves after Him. Meanwhile, let's not forget His promise, "He that believed on me, the works that I do He shall do also."

The healing light of God is unfailing. We can block its radiance with petty thoughts and actions, or we can dismiss thoughts of powerlessness which enables us to have more meaningful demonstrations. This can be accomplished by keeping our focus on the cherished wisdom of Jesus, as our well-being just naturally falls into place. We must be true to the sayings of Jesus and saturate ourselves with them until they are born again in us as faith, the level of which determines the quality of our demonstrations and is in direct proportion to the depth of our devotion.

Jesus revealed the truth about the hidden laws of Mind which are set in motion by faith. Once discovered, we realize we are able to access the mighty reservoirs of creative Mind for the well-being of ourselves and others. We eventually understand, on a deeply intuitive level, we reap precisely what we sow on a moment to moment basis. Is there any one of us who has never said, "I have changed my mind?" This leads us to the conclusion that man and the universe exist in Mind and all changes, for either good or ill, are actually changes of mind.

Jesus revealed the portal to the inner kingdom of mind power. It is readily accessible to us by our meditating upon the life-giving properties of His creative word. We are able to summon the restorative, blissful, peaceful, light and healing current of Spirit emanating from omnipresent God the Father and permeating all that is imperishable.

Jesus was the ultimate wayshower. He succeeded in shepherding us towards a spiritual mindset which set in motion the gradual process of alleviating the mesmerically induced suffering of the

IMAGE № 11 - Christ's Life Depicted in Art

❖

The Sermon on the Mount.
Painting by Carl Bloch.

The Healing Power of Faith

human race. He continues to help those who seek direct union with the spirit of creative mind, as he lovingly proclaimed,

"I am the way and the truth and the life."

Jesus taught that Spirit is the omniscient ruler within. True heroism is born of holding our thoughts on the perfection of the creative power of Spirit, which is made manifest by cause-and-effect, regardless of the hopelessness of outer appearances and beliefs. We must possess a mind that can stand firm in all circumstances, a mind that is brave and heroic. True heroism, being born of firm faith in the eventual expression of good, will supersede all unpleasant conditions caused by erroneous beliefs.

Jesus said, "I and the Father are one," by which He meant when we have spiritually united with creative mind we are able to make our visualizations become realities. It may be we alter our fate by causing that which is God to find expression in word, deed and demonstration. Behind the personal mind is a great creative mind which makes manifest the constructive visualizations we have laid upon the sacred altar of cause-and-effect. We reap precisely what we sow. By trusting in God's presence we become as gods made in His image and likeness. The measure of our power to demonstrate lies in the depth of our faith. Therefore, the visible outer man is that which the inner man constructs with his thoughts.

Jesus was the ultimate practitioner of constructive thinking. He brought to light the fact that humanity unwittingly practices creative visualization, yet for the most part, it is negative due to the myriad erroneous beliefs mankind has become vulnerable to over the course of history. This is what Jesus meant when He said "the truth will set you free." Once we realize we are not powerless victims of circumstance we are able to keep our focus on good rather than evil. We realize good will always triumph over evil when unwavering faith is applied to any given circumstances. "All things whosoever you pray for and ask for, believe that ye receive them and ye shall have them."

Faith is obstructed by ignorance and the unpleasant consequences of cause-and-effect are neutralized by understanding. Sin, which is failing to comply with God's laws, either knowingly or unknowingly, is the Cause and disharmony is the Effect. The mysterious "original sin" is nothing more than unawareness of the existence of the divine laws Jesus came to reveal. When Jesus said, "be as a child," he meant toddlers have not yet been indoctrinated with erroneous race thought and are still pure in heart. His was an enlightening message that caused those who eventually understood it to be forgiven for what were actually sins of omission, with regard to their moral obligations. Joy replaces sorrow, as light replaces darkness when understanding is rewarded with forgiveness of the negative consequences of cause-and-effect.

Most were not ready to accept His message, so they blindly took it out on the messenger. Jesus lessened the suffering of the world with a mastery of truth that continues to redeem humanity from almost certain extinction. He suffered and died for the sole purpose of delivering His redeeming message. I am very grateful to Him being as I think I might have remained in the heavenly realm if faced with the same situation. What would you have done? Just imagine how much He must love us to have voluntarily submitted to such degradation and suffering.

IMAGE # 18 - Christ's Life Depicted in Art

❀

Become as Little Children.
Drawing by Heinrich Hofmann.

The Healing Power of Faith

There are times I think I know how Jesus felt when he said, "My God, why hast thou forsaken me?" Then I realize He actually demonstrated to us that God is always present and is constantly taking form in our lives according to the exact expression of the words, thoughts and deeds, with which we shape our destiny. In his anguish on the cross, he set an example for us to earnestly implore God rather than to lose faith in His power and presence.

We enter the Kingdom of Heaven when we accept the promise of the Scriptures literally, as we look to God for our every need. Jesus said, "all of these things shall be added," to those who earnestly seek the high way of the Lord. Have faith in God in all things and be watchful as good is made manifest. Jesus said, "Ask and you shall receive, seek and ye shall find, knock and it (the kingdom) shall be opened unto you." We love God because He cares for us through the medium of cause-and-effect. We are empowered to demonstrate good in its allness being as we reap precisely what we choose to sow. In Divine Mind all is perfect causation and is waiting to be made manifest in our consciousness merely for the heartfelt asking.

One of the many reasons Jesus came into this world was to uplift humanity by demonstrating life after life. We too have a mission. Unless we find and fulfill our purpose in life we will be destined to search in vain for happiness. If we want to be welcome in heaven we have to dedicate ourselves to being good to others, the reason being in the heavenly realm that's all there is to do. Everyone is kind every moment, otherwise they are no longer welcome to remain in the kingdom.

I suspect that's why we are here in this present life. Like certain archangels, we apparently became self-absorbed and were temporarily banished from the kingdom. Eventually, when we repent, we will be permitted to return. We wonder if there might have been other times we have fallen from our divine, beginningless and endless birthright and where and when else we may have lived a life in total unawareness of our true source. Conversely, some of us may have volunteered our presence here in order to help humanity, as did Jesus. Either way, we pray to be worthy of reentering and thereafter remaining forever, in the bliss of our eternal abode.

Bear in mind literally, the kingdom of heaven is not so much a location, as it is a glorious state of mind which is mutually possessed with all other high-minded souls. Unconditional love manifesting itself in total harmony with the divine mind of God, coupled with The Unfailing Power of Faith are the prerequisites for our eternal individualities to dwell collectively within the sacred society of immortal souls.

"This day you shall be with me in paradise," said Jesus to the repentant thief on Calvary. It appears we are all welcome in heaven once we realize the error of our ways. If you have heard the voice of God and are obedient to Him at any cost, you are chosen. The way into the kingdom will be opened to you.

> "Seek ye first the kingdom of God and
> His righteousness; and all things
> (eternal life) shall be added onto you."

* Inspired by Mark 11:23, Holy Bible   ✤ ✤ ✤

IMAGE № 21 - Christ's Life Depicted in Art

❁

Jesus in the Interiorization of Prayer in Meditation.
Painting by V. V. Sapar.

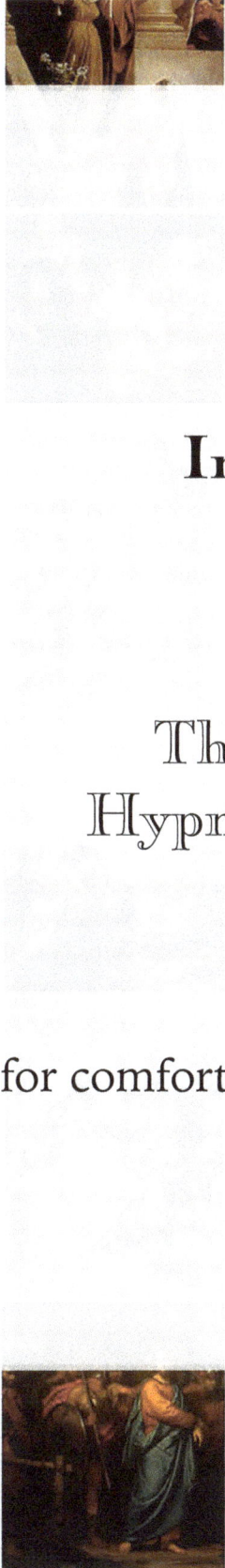

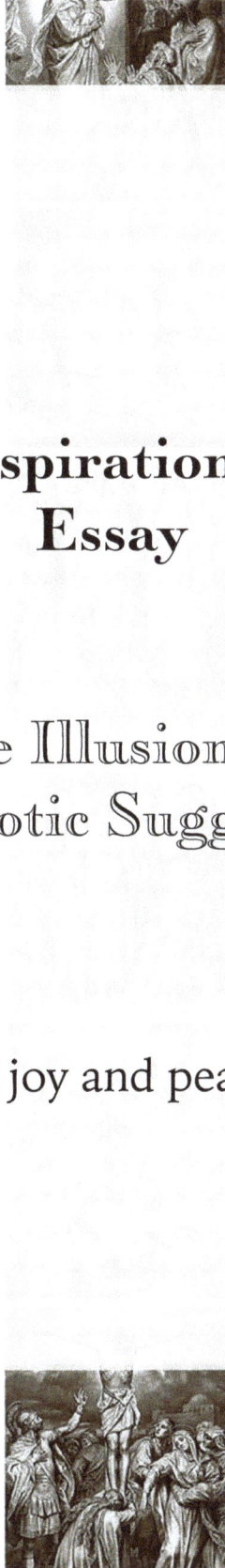

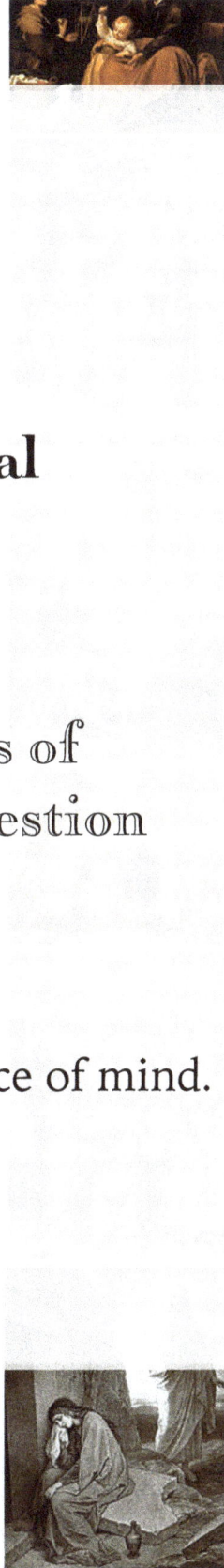

Inspirational
Essay

The Illusions of
Hypnotic Suggestion

for comfort, joy and peace of mind.

The Illusions of Hypnotic Suggestion

A.k.a. Mesmerism or Animal Magnetism

Imagine we are in a hypnotically induced state of mind wherein our thoughts are objectified. There is a mini-personification of illusion sitting on our shoulder trying to influence our human experiences. Fortunately, it lacks the power to permanently induce its materially focused hypnotic suggestions since they are derived entirely from baseless illusions.

On the other shoulder sits a guardian angel imbuing us with the pure ideas of God which empower us to reject the false beliefs of hypnotic suggestion. Consequently, we become increasingly able to establish more and more true ideas in our consciousness, of which the most important, is our likeness to God.

We grow to understand we are perfect expressions of God living an immortal life, this very moment, in a perfectly safe universe. It is only the hypnotic illusion of erroneous beliefs foisted upon us by the collective thoughts of the masses, that keeps us from realizing the Truth.

We overcome material beliefs when we understand them to be the result of the hypnotic illusion of objectified thoughts. The veil of matter will diminish as the grip of illusion is weakened. As the spiritual nature of the universe is increasingly revealed, material beliefs will fade out of consciousness. Hypnotic illusion is all encompassing. Very few people ever think contrary to the prevailing beliefs of the day. Only when one realizes the pervasive nature of hypnotic illusion is there hope of freeing oneself from the unnecessary suffering brought on by our involuntary servitude to destructive hypnotic beliefs.

Our experiences come from either the pure ideas of God or the aggressive mental suggestions gathered by the human mind. Through prayer, spiritual understanding will unfold which will allow us to discern the difference, thereby annihilating worldly hypnotic beliefs, as God's fervently sought intercession blesses us with His purifying ideas.

The reality is "it's all good," with the exception of when we blindly accept what appears to be occurring at the moment with regard to the illusions of matter. Hypnotic suggestion can be compared to a lucid dream. When the dreamer awakens the dream fades into oblivion, along with its various scenarios.

Just as the onset of disease can be induced by a belief implanted by a hypnotist, it follows it can be cured by obliterating the same belief. Under the influence of hypnosis people will acquiesce to the most bizarre circumstances and will behave in a similarly bizarre fashion. They can be made to believe they are animals, or they are impervious to pain, or they are aged or infants, they are wounded or healed, sick or well, weak or strong, cruel or kind, or unreal objects will appear to materialize or vice versa. The scenarios are endless.

In like manner, we are all influenced by different modes of beliefs we inherit from our elders and society in general. Factor in race, color and creed, which create myriad amounts of conflicting cultural differences and hypnotic beliefs become convoluted beyond comprehension. God is the interceding facilitator in terms of our awakening from the erroneous hypnotic beliefs that plague our seemingly treacherous mortal existence.

IMAGE № 17 - Christ's Life Depicted in Art

❈

The Transfiguration.
Painting by Carl Heinrich Bloch.
Courtesy of Det Nationalhistoriske Museum
på Frederiksborg, Hillerød, Denmark.

The Illusions of Hypnotic Suggestion

Is it possible all of humanity is continually being lulled into powerful hypnotic trances within which we believe we are actually experiencing what is being suggested to us? Hopefully, at some point, we will awaken from our trances and realize the unreality of our supposed dilemma. This gives credence to the question, are we personally more affected by hypnotic suggestions than we realize? Are we hypnotized to believe we are powerless victims of circumstance? If we do not feel completely safe in God's care, the answer is an unequivocal yes.

We live in a society that is rampant with suggestion, which suggestion, for the most part, is usually detrimental to our well-being. For instance, the insidious belief in a worrisome disease may be planted deep in our subconscious as a result of fear, which empowers the erring suggestion. It is likely the subconsciously absorbed suggestion that has been impressed on the mind as a belief will be foisted upon us, at some point through the medium of auto-suggestion, which takes the form of predominant thoughts continually revisited. The cause is our thoughts, the effect is their manifestation. Thoughts are cause, which cause beliefs, which bring to fruition seeds planted in fertile mind.

Are vivid impressions sown in our sub-conscious as beliefs? Do they begin to gestate before we reach the age of reason and do they continue to do so throughout our lives? Consider the possibility we may have been taught to believe we are vulnerable to various aggressive hypnotic suggestions. Or, we may have had the misfortune of being inculcated with them as vivid, or as equally damaging, repressed memories. As these beliefs relate to disease, some are considered incurable, or some have varying lesser degrees of seriousness, which prognosis we accept according to the supposed degree of credibility of the source. Jesus summed it up when he said, "Whosoever shall have no doubt in his heart, but believes what he saith will come to pass, he shall have it." Unfortunately, the profoundness of this eternal truth is often sullied by the fact that it is a double edged sword. We reap precisely what we sow, whether it be for good or evil.

That which we truly believe in our hearts will eventually come to the surface demanding some form of resolution, be it either harmonious or inharmonious. We may believe inharmonious circumstances are beyond our control to remedy. Yet, when erroneous hypnotic beliefs are fearlessly resisted with protestations of truth, they must fade away. We must recognize hypnotic suggestions and refuse to believe they are based upon reality, or are more powerful than our ability to shatter them as a result our prayerfully garnered realizations.

Likewise, when Truth is bolstered by fiercely concentrated understanding it flourishes. When we no longer fear a particular detrimental illusion, we have seen the unreality of it, thereby causing it to fade away. We know it is nothing but hypnotic suggestion and as such a hypnotically bound belief. It can be broken by recognizing its inharmonious nature and destroying it with an influx of harmonious realizations of truth. Every resolution of inharmony is based upon our recognizing the fact that whatever can be healed by Love is an expression of the one harmonious Mind of God and Its attributes, of which we are made in His image and likeness.

Is it likely most all of us are unaware of the wide spread influence wielded by hypnotic suggestion? Are disease and death real, or are they bi-products of the illusions of hypnotic suggestion and therefore nonexistent? Have we been lured into the three dimensional world of inharmonious beliefs? Has the fact that we are living in eternity now been obscured? Is it possible to awaken from the illusion of the inharmonious beliefs of disease and death? When the suffering of sin, which is caused

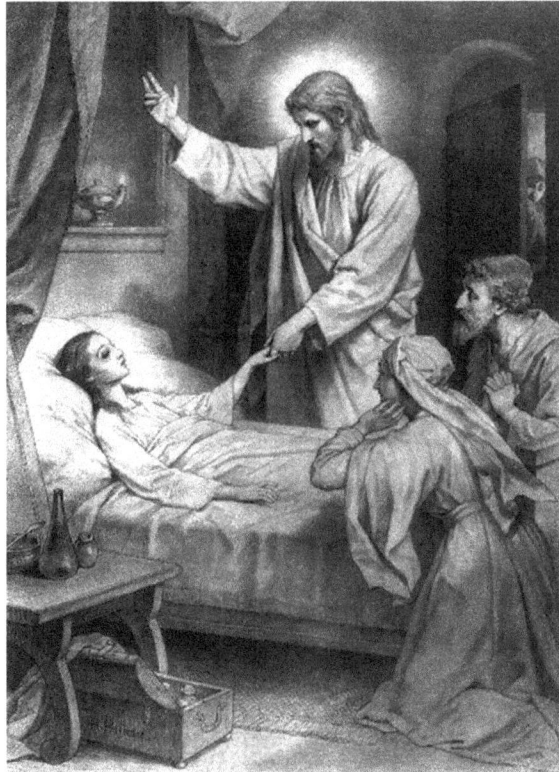

IMAGE № 15 - Christ's Life Depicted in Art

Jesus raises Jairus's Daughter from the Dead.
Drawing by Heinrich Hofmann.

The Illusions of Hypnotic Suggestion

by ignorance of the truth, is shattered by understanding, does the realization that we are living eternal life now, obliterate our self imposed fears?

Was the fall of Adam and Eve and their resultant downward spiral to humanness metaphorical for their succumbing to hypnotically induced beliefs? Was the proverbial forbidden fruit symbolic of those same erring beliefs? Was the allegory of Adam, Eve and the apple indicative of the first ever belief in hypnotic illusion?

Are we forcibly drawn into human consciousness? If so, is the cause our insidious hypnotic beliefs? Do we spend the rest of our seemingly mortal sojourn being buffeted by the winds of hypnotic suggestion? Are we ever quite sure of our divine origin? Did Jesus voice the perfect solution when he said, "Be thou as a child," for it seems the pure in heart see through the illusion of separation from God.

Hypnotic suggestion is a lie. Its weapon is fear. It intercepts the Truth being nourished in mind and replaces it with a belief which cannot be substantiated because there is no reality to it. It is an acquired fear-based belief that fades into oblivion, without a trace of a plausible suggestion remaining, with the onset of the clear evidence of Truth. In the final analysis, our constant task is to vigorously disbelieve our hypnotically induced inharmonious beliefs, no matter how real they appear to be, thereby realizing the unreality of a life apart from the perfection of God. When we revel in God's power and presence we feel Love, in His seeming absence, we feel fear.

We must recognize hypnotic beliefs and refuse to believe there is reality to them. They simply veil the truth. And the truth is, only the pure manifestations of God: Love, Mind, Spirit, Soul, Life, Truth and Principle are harmonious and therefore govern the perfection that is constantly occurring behind the scenes of hypnotic illusion. All that is inharmonious is hypnotic belief and can be dispelled by focusing on the genuine manifestations of Deity.

We love God because he cares for us through the medium of "The Great Law"* of cause-and-effect. It should be thought of as a tool. It is always in operation being as infinite power and intelligence are behind it, not because we need to invoke it. It is self-enforcing as it eradicates all that we resolutely know to be inharmonious. Thanks to The Great Law of cause-and-effect, each time we awaken to the realization that the inherent nature of an inharmonious belief is an illusion (cause), the hypnotic belief reverts back to its natural state of nothingness (effect), corroborating the fact that all that is inharmonious is an illusion and therefore, inherently harmless. In the final analysis, it's either God's distressing absence or His comforting presence that are the measure of the Truth we are able to demonstrate.

Our goal is to realize our oneness with the Father as we partake of His perfection. "The Great Law"* of cause-and-effect is our connection by which we mold our destiny. "It's the source of God's protection, as we believe so we will be."* Our individual happiness blossoms when we realize we have ongoing access to Divinity. We have faith in the protection of God by which He enables us to see through the unreality of hypnotic suggestions and eradicate our discordant beliefs. We love Him because He is our constantly accessible protector.

We are meant to be joyfully aware of the reality of eternal life. We need only purify our minds with elevating thoughts of spiritual understanding in order to free ourselves from the false belief in the

IMAGE № 22 - Christ's Life Depicted in Art

❖

Suffer the Little Children to Come Unto Me.
Drawing by Heinrich Hofmann.

The Illusions of Hypnotic Suggestion

ultimate illusion of death. We thereby usher in the realization of immortality in which every moment of every day is without fear and ultimately timeless, due to our steadfast belief in eternal life. We no longer bear the unbearable weight of intolerable mortality on our shoulders.

We hold the key to happiness in our hands. We can open the flow of the storehouse of joy whenever we desire. Eternal happiness is the result of remaining confident we live within the safety of God's ever protecting love. "Our unwavering trust in God's willingness to enable us to manifest well-being is the catalyst which opens the floodgates of His empowering life force, that which gives light, joy and guidance to our minds and life and healing to our bodies."

We need only to reach the point of realization of "the harmony of being," which Jesus called the Kingdom of Heaven within, where purity abides unceasingly and all is harmonious. Divine Love floods us enlighteningly with Its empowering radiance, once we have rejected the false beliefs of hypnotic illusion and have learned to take refuge in the effulgent light of God's restorative grace. Is this the salvation Jesus promised when He said to the repentant thief on Calvary? "This day you shall be with me in paradise."

God's man is unaffected by the illusions of the human consciousness. He goes about life serenely and confidently. He sees through the false beliefs of matter, which inhibit God's presence, and inner conflict is unknown to him. He navigates effortlessly through evil to good by resolutely invoking the divine ideas of God to enlighten his journey. His faith remains unshakable. He basks in the same life force that gives light, peace and guidance to his thoughts in order to demonstrate increasingly higher reality. He strives continually to elevate his awareness so he may more and more experience a foretaste of permanent immersion in the all encompassing, tranquil world of Spirit.

Jesus demonstrated the unreality of matter by his Ascension. His final demonstration proved his physical body was an illusion as he was gently absorbed into the heavens and disappeared from sight. Do you suppose he was deliberately setting an example for us? After all, he did say, "These things I do, you shall do also and even greater things."**

Visualize a bright and starry night, then imagine it is the Mind of God glowing full orbed within your consciousness. The twinkling stars represent a mere sampling of the myriad amount of God's infinite ideas which are available to us as a result of our realizing our oneness with Him.

Then comes the dawning of illuminating thoughts, whose spiritually awakening ideas reveal a struggling humanity with all its foibles. The prevailing beliefs garnered by humankind seem irrevocable and become painfully ingrained in human consciousness, until such time as we destroy them with the correcting power of Truth. Which Truth is the direct consequence of our ever blossoming understanding, as we blend with the allness of God.

The Illusions of Hypnotic Suggestion www.MyPrayers.net

* Refer to - "The Great Law." by Paul Martin.
** Refer to - "The Imperishable World Beyond." by Paul Martin.

IMAGE № 30 - Christ's Life Depicted in Art

The Resurrection.
Drawing by Heinrich Hofmann.

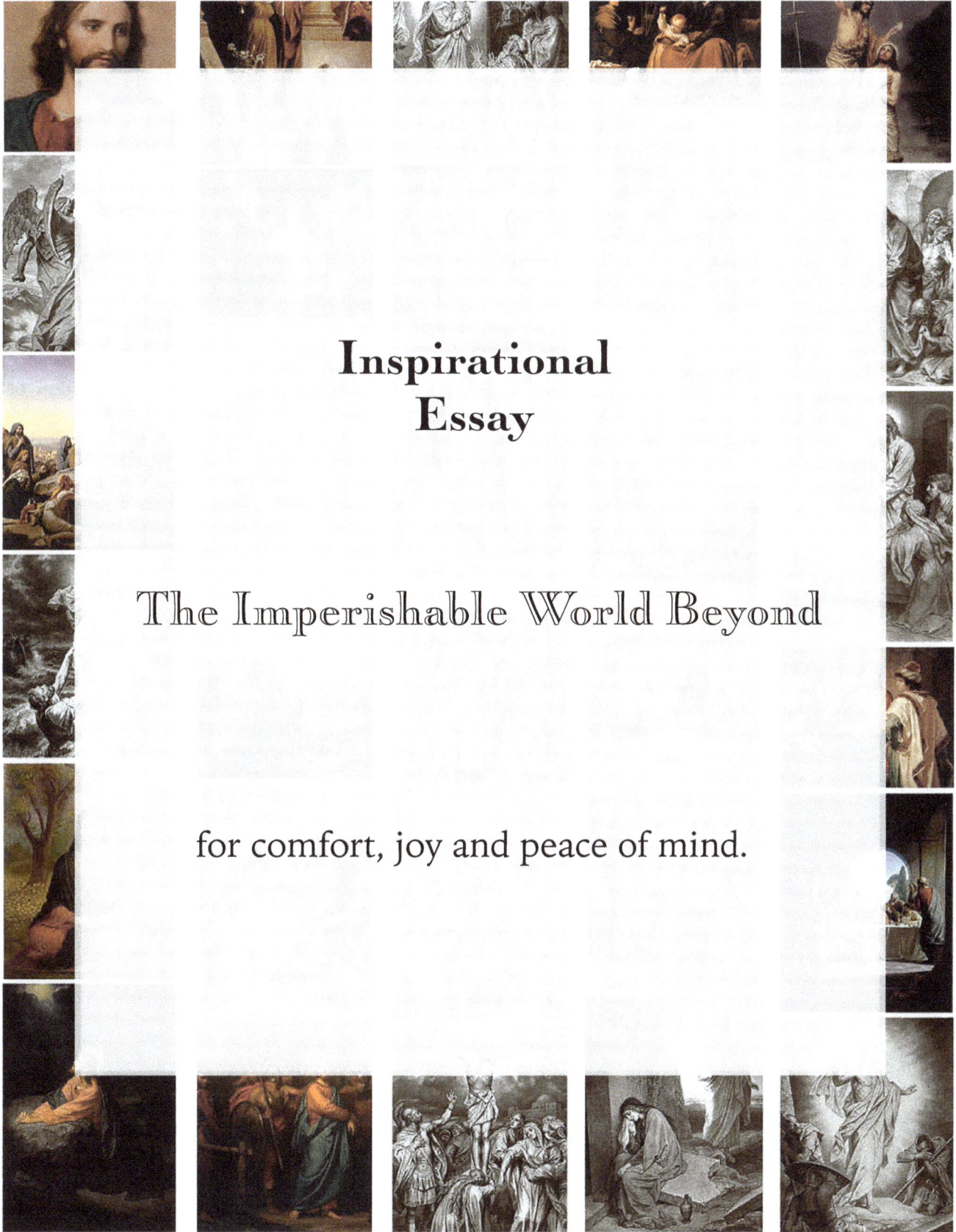

Inspirational Essay

The Imperishable World Beyond

for comfort, joy and peace of mind.

The Imperishable World Beyond

I saw a great light and I was being drawn into it. It emanated warmth and love and was peacefully inviting as it billowed forth from a beckoning tunnel-like passageway, at the end of which stood those I knew and loved. They were motioning to me to come toward them and I was torn between two worlds. The feeling of wanting to go into the light was overwhelming. It was radiantly rainbow hued and brilliantly glistening, yet it did not damage or blind, it accepted, embraced and loved. I felt overwhelmed and overflowing with love and bliss. Gradually my earthly environment faded away and I saw a bright, new and beautiful world of azure skies, opalescent lakes, blossoming meadows, shimmering seas, rainbowed landscapes, perpetual springs, crimson hued sunsets, all beyond my most creative imaginings. I stood in awe and wonder at what could only be described as the world beyond, unimaginably buoyant and beautiful. My new body, which was weightless and made of light, possessed an ease of movement that was fascinatingly mobile. Was I in the realm of eternal life? I looked closely at my arm. It was luminously translucent and reminiscent of glowingly emblazoned objects on a three dimensional movie screen. Everything was a thousand times more vivid and plastic to my thoughts, unfathomably effervescent, lustrous, flowing and surreal, not subject to age or decay.

I felt as though I was in timeless eternity with friends and family from whom I had been temporarily separated. I realized the eternality of love as I reconnected with those loved ones who had arrived before me. Our communications were nonverbal and we felt each other's thoughts deep within our consciousness. Each thought exchanged played little notes within us similar to feelings produced by the sounds and vibrations of softly resonating harp strings. Once again we were drawn together by the bonds of love which had existed between us throughout eternity. All knowledge was instantly and intuitively accessible. Travel was at the speed of thought, for one had only to desire to be in new surroundings and found oneself in the midst of them in an instant. The architectural grandeur was beyond human imagination, being as the materials were constructed and formed with thoughts and therefore limitless in shape and design. Anything one could desire simply had to be conjured into being for we were able to control our surroundings at will. Trees would appear instantly and bore fruit upon request. Children grew to adulthood in a moment simply by willing it to be so. Aging and death were non-existent and everyone was in the prime of their life; young, vibrant, strong, radiant, peaceful, joyous and loving. There was no race, creed or color and we all understood we were created equal and equally loved. I realized I was in familiar surroundings. Had I returned to my true home, no longer a wayward traveler subject to the limiting confines of time and space?

There was an all-pervading awareness of a ubiquitous Supreme Being who was lovingly orchestrating this unfathomable perfection while permeating our every thought and action with the purity that was mercifully flowing from His divine mind through us. We were able to demonstrate this perfection as a result of our unwavering trust in His eternally sheltering love and guidance. This was the prerequisite for our being able to partake of the ever-flowing fountain of truth and immortality which can be so appropriately envisioned as eternal life amidst a harmonious paradise of peace and brotherly love. Our fervent desire was for the blissful unfolding of our perpetually blossoming spiritual awareness.

Like a hand that gives life and movement to a glove, my consciousness had slipped out of my physical body, leaving it seemingly lifeless, inert and sensationless. Could I still return to my earthly habitation

IMAGE № 17 - Christ's Life Depicted in Art

❖

The Transfiguration.
Painting by Carl Heinrich Bloch.
Courtesy of Det Nationalhistoriske Museum
på Frederiksborg, Hillerød, Denmark.

The Imperishable World Beyond

if I wanted to? My desire was to stay here in my newly discovered home. How could I leave this world of magnificent splendor which could be so properly described as being beyond human comprehension? I remembered how I clung to the struggles of life on earth for fear of the unknown. If only I could have been sure what it was like here I would have lived a totally different life, one dedicated to my spiritual growth and the wellbeing of others. I looked down at my physical body through a gently swaying and luminous silver cord which was inconspicuously attached to me by a caressing thought. It all seemed light years away yet the distance presented no difficulty. My human counterpart was lying inertly on my bed where I had left it and I sensed if I willed the silver cord to be broken it would mean the end of life on earth as I knew it. The choice was mine to make. I envisioned loved ones gathered around me grieving for what would seem to them to be the end of my life if I did not return soon. If only they understood I was here and happy and they would see me again before long if I chose not to return. I decided to go back as I realized I had much yet to learn and much reassuring news to return with. Soon my consciousness was merging into my physical body much like a butterfly gently alighting on a motionless blossom, with a "neither here nor there" feeling which was momentarily disconcerting.

I cannot help but wonder which of the two worlds is the real dream. My heavenly sojourn seemed so immeasurably vibrant and real. By comparison, my earthly experience seems so very dull and uncompromising. I wondered if it were possible I had awakened from a dream of mortality for a short time? Could it be our entire physical experience is nothing more than a delusive dream from which we will awaken to find our true home has always been in the imperishable world beyond?

I was in awe and wonder of the indelibly impressed experience I had just undergone. Could it have been a lucid dream or was it a preview of the world beyond? Did I have within me the creativity to conjure up such unfathomably marvelous and mysterious grandeur? Or was I among the privileged few who have been allowed a glimpse of the paradise which was promised by Christ to the repentant criminal who was being crucified beside him on Calvary? "Remember me when you come into your kingdom,"* he humbly asked, and Christ mercifully replied, "This day you shall be with me in paradise."**

 * Refer to - Luke 23:43, Holy Bible
** Refer to - Luke 23:44, Holy Bible

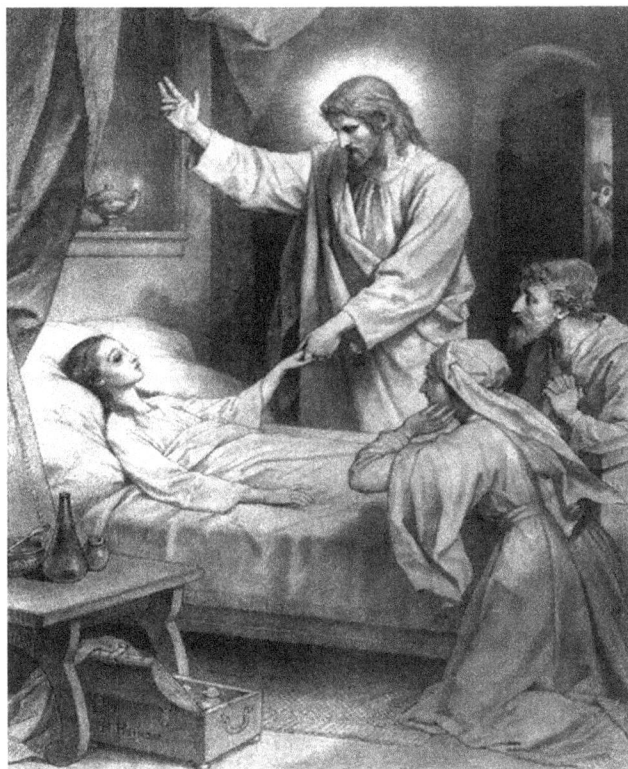

IMAGE № 15 - Christ's Life Depicted in Art

❧

Jesus Raises Jairus's Daughter from the Dead.
Drawing by Heinrich Hofmann.

Inspirational
Essay

The Initiations of Man

for comfort, joy and peace of mind.

The Initiations of Man

The manifestation of the Christ consciousness and our much desired entrance into the Kingdom of God are the immediate tasks ahead, and embody our responsibility, opportunity and destiny. The Initiations by which this transformation occurs are clearly portrayed in the mystical experiences of the Master Jesus during his life on Earth, and are known as Birth, Baptism, Crucifixion, Resurrection and Ascension. As we pass through these enlightening portals we are able to follow in the Master's footsteps. These upwardly ascending rites of passage are both actual and metaphorical and provide continually blossoming awareness to the disciple as he struggles to make his way toward the proverbial light at the end of the tunnel.

The existence and relevance of these initiations were demonstrated by Christ and Master Jesus, and exemplify the advancement of the humanly garbed soul as it passes through the stages of its spiritual journey and is faced with the trials and tribulations associated with blessedly unfolding expansions of consciousness. This knowledge is of great value and service to the aspirant on the path of spiritual awakening, to realize the experiences of the Master Jesus, including that of the Crucifixion and the Resurrection, are reflected through the lives of all living beings. As the Christ principle unfolds in our heart and consciousness, we all must walk the Way of the Cross eventually to become soul-illumined sons of God. Whether or not we are aware of the spiritual journey before us, all men ascend from one spiritual plateau to another on the wings of these mandatory and progressively enlightening paths of spiritual evolution.

At some point along the way of our long and arduous journey a call to service will beckon to the devoted seeker. We will learn to serve as Christ served, to love all men as he loved them, and by the strength of our spiritual dedication and the quality of our service, inspire all we meet so they too can serve, love and become members of the Kingdom. The need is for dedicated men and women who can understand the necessity of doing all they can possibly do in order to make their own unique contribution toward the uplifting and liberation of humanity. These dedicated servants devote their lives to expressing to the world the qualities of the citizens of the Kingdom of immortal souls: love, wisdom, kindness, compassion, uncompromising involvement and spiritually based freedom of hearts and minds.

Birth, the awareness of consciousness. **Baptism,** the initial experience with God-union which creates the desire to devote oneself fully to pursuing the spiritual path. **Crucifixion,** the overcoming of delusion through higher awareness so the Christ consciousness may be more fully expressed. **Resurrection,** the gradual restoring of our hearts and minds to "childlike" purity. **Ascension,** the progressive unfolding of man's spiritual nature toward increasingly broader visceral awareness which is the catalyst for deeper communion with God.

Transfiguration is the highest, all encompassing and voluntarily attainable Initiation. A supernatural glow takes place when one's thought has progressed to the point where the full force of divine Mind flows through his being. With regard to great Masters it is preordained; for the advanced devotee it can be achieved through unbridled and unrelenting dedication. Transfiguration was demonstrated by Masters of Christ's, Buddha's, Krishna's, and Moses' stature, and many others throughout the course of humanity. Not by coincidence, all Masters possess the Christ Consciousness by which they

Agony in the Garden.
Painting by Carl Bloch.

The Initiations of Man

express the qualities of love, peace, light, purity, joy, guilelessness, innocence, obedience, humbleness, meekness, trust, bliss, wisdom and lack of egotism, body consciousness, selfishness and attachment. They have a super-conscious awareness of God's omniscience, omnipresence and omnipotence and their own ability to serve as a conduit to manifest these divine powers for the benefit of mankind. Only when we become possessed of these qualities through prayer, meditation and selfdiscipline can we prepare ourselves to receive and manifest Christ Consciousness and demonstrate Transfiguration.

Your notes

_____

_____

_____

_____

_____

_____

_____

_____

_____

_____

_____

Inspirational Essay

The Lord's Prayer - A Guide to experiencing the blissful presence of God.

for comfort, joy and peace of mind.

The Lord's Prayer – A Guide
to experiencing the blissful presence of God.

Forward

If you are stumbling hopelessly around in a dark room, is it reasonable to assume all you would have to do to end your misery is to turn on the light? Does the light know anything about your difficulties, or is it in any way responsible? Or is it the absence of light which has caused the problem? Jesus' purpose in creating The Lord's Prayer was to show us the way to elevate ourselves above the despair of emotional darkness by taking steps to allow the joyful, healing and redeeming Guiding Light of Christ, emanating from God the Father, into our consciousness. The choice to experience this loving and blissful presence is ours to make on a moment to moment basis.

A Guide to experiencing the blissful presence of God.

Jesus gave us The Lord's Prayer.
It is the summation of all His teachings.

The Lord's Prayer was intended to make us aware of the existence of God's unalterable laws of cause and effect and the importance of conforming to them. It is the spiritual key to opening our hearts and minds to God's empowering Love. It would be highly improbable anyone other than one of Jesus' spiritual perfection could live in perfect harmony with creation's governing laws as expressed by the Spirit of God through the Christ Consciousness. To continually strive to understand these laws and to endeavor to conform to them is a monumental and empowering, ongoing quest, which will eventually lead us to establish communion with the peace, love and healing presence of God. Jesus possessed the Christ Consciousness in all its effulgence and was the Guiding Light sent by God the Father to lead us out of the wilderness of delusion. His purpose was to help us to understand mortal life is governed by God's unalterable laws of cause and effect and the Soul of man, being a reflection of transcendent Spirit, is above the subjugation of cause and effect. He bore witness to the fact that the Spirit of God is the creator and the breath of all life and is the governing, guiding, restoring, correcting, purifying, life-giving essence of the infallible laws governing the life and intelligence in all that is now, ever was, or ever will be. The source of Jesus' miraculous powers was his perfect alignment with God's governing laws which enabled him to be a mercifully empowered conduit between God and man.

Thus did Jesus counsel: "Seek ye first the kingdom of God (rise above the insidious power of delusion) and all else (the fulfillment of man's deepest desire to know God, and the resultant healing of body, mind and soul) will be added unto you (according to your divine birthright as a child of God)."

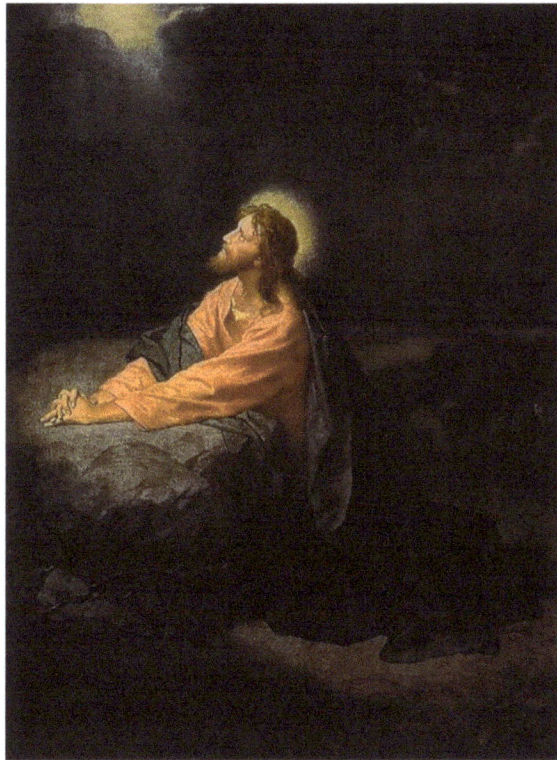

IMAGE № 26 - Christ's Life Depicted in Art

❀

Jesus Praying in the Garden of Gethsemane.
Painting by Heinrich Hofmann.

The Lord's Prayer – A Guide
to experiencing the blissful presence of God.

Our Father

We are children of God,
created equal and equally loved.

Jesus said, "Is it not written in your law, I said, ye are gods?" He saw God in all. He wanted us to know Divinity expresses itself as the individual identities within the divine temples of our Souls. When we realize this we take an important step toward conforming to God's unalterable laws of cause and effect. The highest commandments are to love God with all your heart, with all your Soul, with all your mind, and secondly, to love thy neighbor as thyself. If we are the least little bit prejudiced, or if we have feelings of superiority or inferiority, we bring disturbing thoughts upon ourselves that block our receptivity to God. To find God and to allow Him into our hearts, the first requirement is to love Him with the same intense and comforting love we feel for those who are nearest and dearest to us. If we actually feel Love which springs from gratitude for the Almighty we will have no choice but to love all His children equally, for we will be loving the Divinity within each and every person. Do we really love God and understand all He does for us when we conform to His laws? If we truly understand the precise degree He responds to our thoughts and actions, we would have no greater desire than to love Him and no greater love for anyone or anything. The gratitude we express to God and our fellow beings is a pure expression of Love and is returned to us precisely in kind. In His impartiality He made all Souls alike and in His image. When we fail to recognize and love the Divinity in others, we misuse our God-given independence and bring retributive, yet lawful results upon ourselves as we reap precisely what we have sown. If we do not feel love equally for all, we will not be receptive to Love in general and we will suffer the despair of being disconnected from God. As He is constant, so should we be constant in expressing our love to others and to the Divinity within them. We should take every prudent opportunity to exchange a heartfelt smile, which expresses a kind thought, with all who come our way. We should cherish our friendships and strive to nourish them with kindness and understanding, for friendships are the highest form of love as they make no demands.

IMAGE № 22 - Christ's Life Depicted in Art

❁

Suffer the Little Children to Come Unto Me.
Drawing by Heinrich Hofmann.

The Lord's Prayer – A Guide
to experiencing the blissful presence of God.

which art in heaven,

We are eternally immersed in mercifully empowering Infinite Love, Life and Truth.

Like a fish is immersed in water we are immersed in the invisible ocean of eternal and omnipresent Cosmic Consciousness. God expects us to attune our lives to His ubiquitous infinite Love, Life and Truth, which are the foundation of the Divine laws by which all that rightfully exists is governed. The sun, the moon, the stars, the trees, the plants, the animals, all have an obvious intelligence and know what to do and when to do it. Being as they are not endowed with free will they function perfectly well yet will never be any more or less than they currently are. Mankind is governed by the same intelligent life force, yet being as we have free will, we are often out of harmony with Divine Mind due to the wrong choices we make. Nonetheless, it is this same free will that allows us to grow in spiritual awareness throughout eternity. Unfortunately, if it is not used wisely, it can work to our detriment. Therefore the choices we make determine the quality of our eternal life and account for the amount of, or lack of progress we make. Man differs from any other creature being as he is endowed with potentially unlimited awareness. "Mercifully empowering" means that God in His infinite mercy gives us ever increasing insights and prophetic visions with which to purify our thoughts and actions and as a result, we are able to maintain dominion over our inner and outer worlds. We become increasingly able and willing to conform to His unalterable laws of cause and effect. We turn on His empowering life current by means of our exalted thoughts and actions. We create fullness of life by refusing to allow doubtful and faithless thoughts and actions to block the beneficial flow of the universal Christ Consciousness. We continue to immerse ourselves in the Truth with regard to the responsive nature of God, which blossoms into an intuitive awareness of the unreality of all that is not God-centered. We become as little children, safe in our Father-Mother God's loving bosom throughout eternity. We realize He is always with us and is constantly creating our lives according to the precise expression of our thoughts, words and actions. When we raise our expectations to the level of God's love for us, we acquire the power to demonstrate over all manner of difficulties. We reap the untold blessings of His eternally sheltering love and guidance.

IMAGE № 18 - Christ's Life Depicted in Art

❦

Become as Little Children.
Drawing by Heinrich Hofmann.

The Lord's Prayer - A Guide
to experiencing the blissful presence of God.

Hallowed be Thy name.

Thy loving perfection is unfathomably worthy of humble and devoted adoration.

"Thou shalt love the Lord thy God with all thy heart, with all thy Soul and all thy mind" would be much easier to demonstrate if we understood the profound and responsive nature of God, what our relationship to Him is and what is the extent of the power He places at our disposal. Jesus created The Lord's Prayer for this reason. He wanted us to understand God and as a result, when we focus our thoughts on Him in spiritual contemplation, we will be correcting all the worldly misconceptions by which we are continually led to make undesirable choices in our lives. We will become more capable of opening the aperture, that creates the illusion of separateness from God, which allows His love, bliss, wisdom and healing presence to flow into us. The deeper meaning of prayer is not in asking for specific requests but rather to revel in the fruits of blissful and enlightening God-communion and resultant wisdom. This automatically corrects all our difficulties in life, some of which we are aware of and some which we are not. We must never place more faith in someone or something other than God or we will violate the first Commandment which will block us from His love, protection and empowerment. The workings of cause and effect are simple: The more we are attuned to God's laws the more we can experience His love, guidance and protection. What one must do to rise above the human condition is to continually trust in God and to turn to Him unceasingly. No longer will we be looking for Love in all the wrong places. To achieve salvation is to experience the presence of God and to understand all that is available to us by virtue of his nurturing love throughout eternal life. We will have learned to use the power and the wisdom so magnanimously bestowed upon us for the benefit of ourselves as well as for others.

IMAGE № 11- Christ's Life Depicted in Art

The Sermon on the Mount.
Painting by Carl Bloch.

The Lord's Prayer – A Guide
to experiencing the blissful presence of God.

Thy kingdom come.

Exalted thoughts open us
to the ever-flowing love of God.

Jesus counseled "Ask and you shall receive." Whatever we ask for which is for the common good of all, we will receive. Likewise, if it is not for the good of all, it will be not in conformance with God's laws of cause and effect and is therefore a wrong request. When we steadfastly deliberate about what we understand the nature of God to be and pray only for knowledge of His will for us we will open the portals of heavenly God-sent wisdom which will be bestowed upon us through intuition and prophetic visions. Within this wisdom will be the knowledge of what is right and wrong in God's eyes. His kingdom of peace, love, joy and healing presence will then be able to flow into our hearts and minds. In reality this precious God-communion should be our only request. All else can be left in God's hands as we trust in His eternally sheltering love and guidance. We can develop the spiritually enriching courage that results from remaining poised and God-centered amidst the many dangers, toils and snares by which we are continually challenged. Instead of life becoming more difficult as it progresses, it gets more rewarding as our understanding of God and his empowering blessings continues to blossom into dominion over difficulties that were previously thought to be insurmountable.

IMAGE № 2 - Christ's Life Depicted in Art

❖

Mary Visits the Mother of John the Baptist.
Painting by Carl Bloch.

The Lord's Prayer – A Guide
to experiencing the blissful presence of God.

Thy will be done

We are unceasingly enlightened by God's unalterable laws of cause and effect.

God's will is expressed and witnessed to by His unalterable laws of cause and effect which either reward or correct us according to that which we have created by our own thoughts and actions. The highest reward we can receive which indicates we are in tune with the divine mind of God is to experience Him as love, light, peace and joy and healing presence, as well as divine guidance. Any discord in our life is the direct result of our erroneous thinking and can be corrected as quickly as we can raise our consciousness to the point where we are willing to sacrifice our self-centered ways for the higher goal of attaining God's love, protection and empowerment. For those who have not experienced communion with God, it should be taken on faith that it is possible to do so from the many who have. A constant vigilance is required in order to maintain inner-communion on a meaningful level, and also to maintain the constant dedication necessary to see this blissful relationship blossom to continually more rewarding depths. The reality is there is not one single moment when the laws of cause and effect are not being demonstrated by man as a result of his thoughts and actions. We conform to or violate God's unalterable laws primarily through our thoughts which are the root cause of our actions. We can choose to focus on creating good thoughts and their resultant good actions, for the benefit of ourselves and as well as for others. God's unalterable laws can be made to work for the benefit of man but they cannot be transcended except by God himself, or by one who has established inner-communion with Him. When one disregards the dictates of conscience they become disconnected from their inner world of harmony with God and suffer the consequences of their misguided choices.

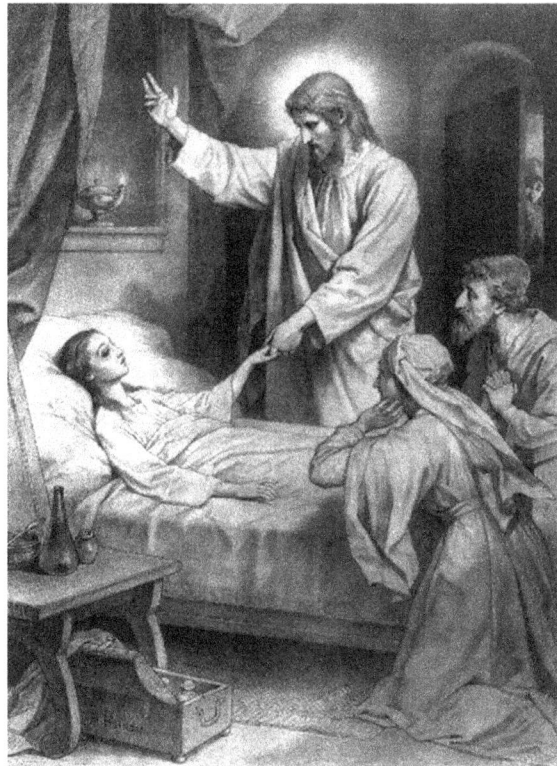

IMAGE № 15 - Christ's Life Depicted in Art

✤

Jesus Raises Jairus's Daughter From the Dead.
Drawing by Heinrich Hofmann.

The Lord's Prayer – A Guide
to experiencing the blissful presence of God.

in earth, as it is in heaven.

Exalted thoughts find expression according to our understanding of and adherence to spiritual laws.

In order for us to reap the ultimate blessings of God's unalterable laws of cause and effect, it is helpful to understand how these laws affect us and then try to live in harmony with them. We must continually stand guard over our errant thoughts and actions in order that we can make meaningful demonstrations of the unlimited power and protection provided by divine decree. To the degree we can conform to and thereby implement these God-given, mercifully empowering divine laws, we will eventually realize everything we perceive to be reality is beneficially moldable and adaptable to our thoughts. We do not have to approach God as beggars for what is rightly ours in accordance with His divine laws. We are always in a position to gratefully expect what we are entitled to as a result of our adherence to His unalterable laws of cause and effect. We should pray continually for the wisdom to understand His will and for the courage, unselfishness and perseverance to conform to His divine government. Eventually we realize the Soul of man, being the son of God and a reflection of transcendent Spirit, is above the subjugation of cause and effect. When we are identified with our assumed mortal identity, the laws of cause and effect reward us only in accordance with our earned merits. One who is consciously identified with the Spirit within reaps the infinite richness of Divinity which supersedes the encumbrances of mortal limitations.

IMAGE № 21 - Christ's Life Depicted in Art

✿

Jesus in the Interiorization of Prayer in Meditation.
Painting by V. V. Sapar.

The Lord's Prayer – A Guide
to experiencing the blissful presence of God.

Give us this day our daily bread;

God soothes us with the loving light of Grace
as our needs are supplied through unlimited sources.

God intercedes for us in order to forgive the negative cosmic consequences of cause and effect. We are rewarded for the understanding of and repentance for our violations of His unalterable laws. As a direct result of establishing an inner harmonious connection with God, we eventually develop an unwavering awareness of eternal life. His blissful presence may be considered the ultimate expression of Grace and is bestowed on us through His tender guidance and beneficence. Therefore, when we repent, as a result of understanding what we have done wrong, God forgives us and alleviates our suffering by rewarding us with His blissful presence. He soothes us with the continual awareness of eternal life as He supplies our needs through different and sometimes unexpected sources. These sources may take the form of people helping us whom we would least expect to do so. We may receive unexpected opportunities or lastly, unexpected spiritual insights that lift us above worldly conditions so we may soar with the angels in a way we never dreamed possible. The reality is, what we "reap" is the precise and direct result of what we "sow." Therefore, there are no victims. God rewards us with the Amazing Grace of His loving and blissful presence to the degree we conform to His unalterable laws of cause and effect. We do not have to settle for simply neutralizing unhappy occurrences in our lives. We can tip the scales in our favor by thinking and doing a preponderance of good and thereby reaping the favorable results. We can allow the wisdom of Spirit to guide all our thoughts and actions in order that we may align ourselves with God's governing laws.

IMAGE № 10 - Christ's Life Depicted in Art

❧

Healing the Sick.
Drawing by Heinrich Hofmann.

The Lord's Prayer - A Guide
to experiencing the blissful presence of God.

And forgive us our debts,

Joy replaces sorrow as light replaces darkness
when understanding is rewarded with forgiveness.

When we understand what we have done wrong we see the light both literally and figuratively. We are forgiven by the Grace of God and as a result the retribution, in the form of His absence, that was meted out by His laws of cause and effect is nullified. When Jesus healed the sick he said, "Your sins are forgiven thee." Had he raised the consciousness of those individuals in order to annul the retribution that was the root cause of their illness? Accordingly, we must be willing to examine ourselves in order to decide objectively if we are in violation of God's laws. When we truly realize "we reap what we sow," we become willing to take responsibility for our thoughts and actions and in doing so we take the first step toward being forgiven. His wisdom shines on the darkness of erroneous beliefs that were creating our inability to be attuned to Him in spiritual contemplation. Our sorrow is replaced by the joy of being able to experience God-communion and to avail ourselves of His many empowering blessings. The light of Truth will shine on the darkness of erroneous thoughts and delusive beliefs and cause them to disappear, much as the night disappears with the coming of the dawn. When an expansive and redeeming awareness dawns on us, the God-sent Guiding Light of Christ will eradicate the darkness and suffering caused by our unwitting violations of His unalterable laws of cause and effect. Therefore, God is both law and Love, yet Love transcends law as law can be set aside by Love.

The God seeking individual, by prayerfully intuitive perception, explores the depths of his Soul and gathers all offensive tendencies which are methodically consumed by the flames of fiery wisdom. The innate purity of each of us devoted to Truth emerges from behind the clouds of delusion and shines forth as the eradicating sun of wisdom. For those who possess spiritual readiness, let them experience Truth through the direct perception of purifying and enlightening Intuition. So it is, when we realize the error of our ways, we are forgiven. We are purified by eternally blossoming understanding. Joy replaces sorrow, as light replaces darkness, when understanding is rewarded with forgiveness.

IMAGE № 9 - Christ's Life Depicted in Art

✦

Jesus and the Woman of Samaria.
Drawing by Heinrich Hofmann.

The Lord's Prayer - A Guide
to experiencing the blissful presence of God.

as we forgive our debtors.

Understanding enables us to forgive
and rewards us with peace.

When we have a grievance with someone, the absence of understanding, which would allow us to forgive, clouds our thoughts with the unhappiness of the false emotion of anger and the underlying emotion of fear. We suffer emotional pain as a result of being blocked from experiencing God's love, light, joy, wisdom and healing presence. When we understand all people are good people who behave badly at times, we are able to forgive. As a result of the understanding that leads to forgiveness we are rewarded with peace of mind which is a prerequisite for experiencing God-communion. The reality is everyone is basically good and we must love all equally. We may not like their behavior at times, but we must continue to honor the Divinity within them. We must realize "To err is human and to forgive is Divine." The same understanding we extend to others will allow us to understand our own shortcomings and be forgiven. In this regard, Jesus set a lofty standard for us to aspire to. While enduring the physical pain and agony of crucifixion, he did not want to add to his suffering by allowing himself to feel the mental anguish of anger and fear that would have surely separated him from communion with God. This apparently occurred for a few moments when he cried out, "My God why hast thou forsaken me?" Did he assuage his doubt when he looked up to the heavens and said, "Father, forgive them for they know not what they do?" Could this have been the antidote for his mental anguish? Jesus asked the Father to expunge the retribution that would be meted by the laws of cause and effect to those who were crucifying him. Not only did Jesus forgive his persecutors but he prayed that they, who dealt out such merciless and heartbreaking cruelty to him, would not suffer a similar fate. He knew they did not understand the hideousness of their unwarranted persecution of him and he lovingly forgave them, as he prayed for their redemption. He asked the Father to raise their consciousness so their sins, which were a manifestation of their ignorance, would be forgiven. In doing so he set a transformative example for us to follow, as he demonstrated how to free one's self, through forgiveness, from the paralyzing grip of the painfully destructive emotions of anger and fear. The Truth had set Jesus free and it will set us free as well. We will be rewarded with the peace that emanates from and surpasses all understanding.

IMAGE № 20 - Christ's Life Depicted in Art

❖

Christ and the Rich Young Ruler.
Painting by Heinrich Hofmann.
Courtesty of The Riverside Church, New York City
and New York Graphic Society.

The Lord's Prayer – A Guide
to experiencing the blissful presence of God.

And lead us not into temptation,

Our infinite capacity for spiritual expansion
is enhanced by harmonious thoughts and actions.

We can ask God to help us to avoid the dark unsettling emotions created by doubtful and faithless thoughts and actions that block us from His love, light, intuitive guidance, peace and joy. When we become aware that we have an infinite capacity for spiritual expansion we do not want to waste one thought or action on anything other than what has the power to expand our consciousness. We recognize that our spiritual progress hinges on the moment to moment choices we make throughout our lives. Consequently, we would rather our spiritual evolution be more rapid and be the direct result of pleasant, rather than the painful retributive learning experiences meted out by the laws of cause and effect as a direct result of God's absence in our lives. The more we can expand our understanding, the more blissful we will be as we become increasingly able to transcend our self-imposed limitations. We are able to take blissful refuge in the beckoning and effulgent bosom of Spirit.

IMAGE № 7 - Christ's Life Depicted in Art

The Boy Jesus with the Doctors in the Temple.
Painting by Heinrich Hofmann.

The Lord's Prayer - A Guide
to experiencing the blissful presence of God.

but deliver us from evil;

Our thoughts and actions
are purified by illuminating intuition.

God delivers us from doubtful and faithless thoughts and actions by speaking to us through intuition and prophetic visions. His awakening Grace is granted to us incrementally and only to the degree we are ready to receive His rewarding and spiritually expansive enlightenment. He waits for us to be receptive so He can whisper words of wisdom to us as a loving Mother or Father would speak to their beloved child. He awakens us patiently as He waits for us to implement His guidance. We are delivered from suffering and evil as He guides us to comply with His unalterable laws of cause and effect. As a result we are able to avoid the correcting ill-effects created by His absence, which are the underlying causes of all of our difficulties. Our Souls are incrementally redeemed from the ignorance born of delusion, which causes us to forget our Divine nature and to be absorbed in our vulnerable human nature. As we grow in spiritual awareness, we increasingly perceive the enlightening nature of Christ's teachings and their inherent ability to make us aware; the unfathomable nature of God is expressed through eternal Love, forgiveness and redeeming guidance. It is only when we realize our unworthiness to receive God's blessings in totality do we begin to tread the spiritually expansive, homeward-bound path of discipleship.

IMAGE № 22 - Christ's Life Depicted in Art

❦

Suffer the Little Children to Come Unto Me.
Dawing by Heinrich Hofmann.

The Lord's Prayer – A Guide
to experiencing the blissful presence of God.

For Thine is the kingdom,
and the power, and the glory,

God is omnipresent,
omnipotent and omniscient.

For Thine is the Kingdom, the Power and the Glory refers to the Divine laws which are the perfect expression of God's harmonious rule as they ubiquitously permeate everything, everywhere and are limitless and all powerful. They demonstrate God's scientific perfection which is the cohesive force within all that is seen and all that is unseen, in this and all the worlds beyond. These unifying laws are the expression of God's perfect will. They are constantly adjusting and correcting for the betterment of everyone and everything, including all that takes place in thought and action. For every thought and action there is a precise and divinely orchestrated reaction which is the purifying force within all that exists and all that is eternal. All who faithfully seek His eternally sheltering love and guidance, by bringing their thoughts and actions into harmony with His Divine laws, will surely experience the purifying and expansive, sacred, blissful and healing presence of our almighty Creator. Therefore, God is everywhere present, all powerful and precisely scientific.

If in fact God is everywhere present He cannot possibly be a detached deity sitting on a throne in some inaccessible location. Is it possible He reaches out to the sinners (those who are unaware of, or are unwilling to conform to His laws), counsels those who labor for higher consciousness and rejoices with those who experience the innate bliss of the Soul? Is He within us all forever whether or not we feel His presence? Does salvation lie in destroying the illusion of individualism which separates us from the blissful power and protection of our beneficent Creator?

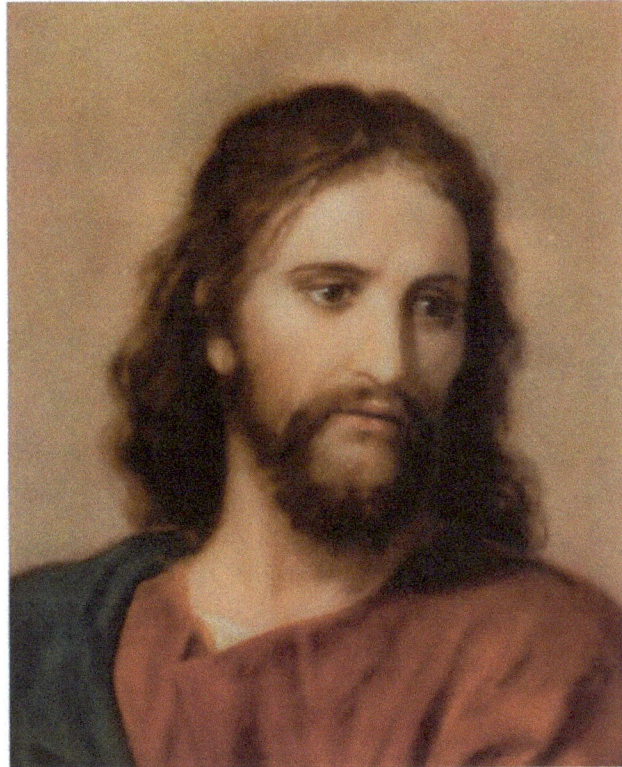

IMAGE № 1 - Christ's Life Depicted in Art

Christ at 33.
Painting by Heinrich Hofmann.

The Lord's Prayer – A Guide
to experiencing the blissful presence of God.

forever. Amen.

We trust in God's eternally sheltering love and guidance.

Herein is represented the essence of spirituality and embodies the spirit of Christ's teachings. "We" signifies humanity as being all of God's children created equally and equally loved. "Trust" is the essential ingredient of faith, the cornerstone of hope and the process of spiritual evolution by which we progress from blind faith and baseless hope to spiritual conviction gained through understanding. When we trust in God's eternally sheltering love and guidance we take comfort in his infinite protection. We lift the veil of delusion that separates us from the peace, joy and healing presence of God within us. To be sheltered and protected from life's continual onslaughts is an immeasurable blessing. To be eternally guided through prayerfully acquired and magnanimously bestowed intuition is to find solace in the God-given awarenesses that allow us to navigate the often treacherous and unchartered waters of life. We are able to gravitate effortlessly toward the peace and serenity of His sheltering love. Whoever wholeheartedly desires the tender protection of Almighty God will be unceasingly enlightened by the infinite wisdom of divinely granted intuition. The "second birth," the necessity of which Jesus spoke, admits us to the land of intuitive perception of God's will. Through our illumined comprehension we can enter the Cosmic Consciousness of the Kingdom of God, the eternal abode of ever purifying Truth and eternally limitless Souls.

Absolute unquestioning trust in God is the greatest method of instantaneous healing of body (son of man) and Soul (son of God). An increasing effort to arouse that trust is man's highest and most rewarding duty. There is nothing more satisfying than wisdom and truth and the truth is we are eternally safe in God's loving care and guidance.

IMAGE № 19 - Christ's Life Depicted in Art

❁

Christ with Mary and Martha.
Painting by Heinrich Hofmann.
Courtesy of Stadtmuseum Bautzen, Germany.

The Lord's Prayer – A Guide
to experiencing the blissful presence of God.

The Guiding Light of Christ

The Guiding Light of Christ, emanating from God the Father, is eternally present in our Souls. We can awaken our hearts and minds to experience the light in a rewarding and meaningful way. The voice of our conscience is the voice of God. It adheres to the truth of the intuitive wisdom within. One can detect when a wrong choice, in either thought or action, has been made by the uneasiness and inner disturbance it creates within us. Virtue is recognizable by the inner harmony it engenders. The Guiding Light is always present and offering us discriminative wisdom which is recognizable by the calm and peaceful feelings it creates. If one does not block their discriminative wisdom by rationalizing wrong behavior and disregarding one's conscience, they will be led by The Guiding Light. To follow the light of inner guidance is to tread the path of ever increasing awareness. We disengage from the Soul shrouding influence of wrong choices that overshadow our discriminative power to define right from wrong actions. The constant seeker of The Guiding Light gradually transcends his habit bound worldly ways. He is increasingly baptized in the light of Christ wisdom. He is born anew as a partaker of the unerring guidance of The Guiding Light within. He experiences the heavenly vision of God's all-knowing wisdom as he devotedly gravitates toward ultimate oneness with the ubiquitous mind of the heavenly Father, as expressed through the redeeming light of the Christ Consciousness. God is the eternal fountain and the source of all that is good and true and all that is good and true is made manifest by the purifying waters of the Christ Consciousness.

Your
notes

_____

_____

_____

_____

_____

_____

_____

_____

_____

_____

Inspirational
Essay

Thomas Jefferson's Secret Life

for comfort, joy and peace of mind.

Thomas Jefferson's Secret Life

I was born in 1743 and I completed The Declaration of Independence in 1776 when I was thirty three years old. I passed away on July 4th 1826 at the age of eight three, exactly 50 years to the day of its signing. The phrase "All men are created equal and are endowed with certain inalienable rights, among these being life, liberty and the pursuit of happiness" was something I had to struggle to include, as the founding fathers were very much opposed to it. I wanted this central truth to be more specific, "All men, women and children regardless of race, color or creed." After much intense negotiation I had to settle for the former generic meaning although this pronouncement has long since been considered to be the most well- known sentence ever written in the English language. For the most part of my adult life I owned many slaves, one of which would eventually become my dearest confidant and lifelong companion. Her name was Sally Hemings (1773-1835). Needless to say this was quite a contradiction. This is our story and I hope to shed light on it. Sally and I had six children together who were considered to be of mixed race, four of which survived to maturity. She was the second and last women I would ever love.

When my wife Martha and I were married she came to live with me at my beloved plantation home Monticello. Upon her father's passing shortly thereafter, she inherited all his many slaves and a large property of some 1300 acres which comprised his plantation. Sally Hemings was one of Martha's six young slave siblings who came to live with us along with their half white slave mother Elizabeth. They were actually Martha's half brothers and sisters being they had the same father. Although personal relationships between whites and blacks could not be acknowledged in those days, Martha loved these siblings dearly and did not want to be separated from them. For this reason they came to live with us. Sally eventually grew to be a beautiful, well-spoken woman who was the haunting image of my dear wife Martha who had passed away at the untimely age of thirty three. I loved Mrs. Jefferson deeply and I felt my life was over without her. Ironically, on her death bed, she made me promise never to remarry and as things turned out it was a promise I could not break, even if I wanted to and I did eventually want to. I am sure Martha would have wanted me too as well, given the circumstances which I will relate to you now.

In those days we cherished every moment of life and equally so those we loved, being as we all had much firsthand experience as to the fragility of life. We tried to have as many children as possible for that was the only way we could be assured of having a few survive to maturity and eventually be fortunate enough to have children and possibly grandchildren to protect and care for us in our later years. We lived at a period in time when the average life expectancy was in the mid-thirties due to many diseases which have long since been eradicated. Only two of Martha's and my six children lived to maturity and one died at the age of 25. Only our daughter Patsy survived me.

I was, in all sincerity, a spiritually minded and moral person. I believed in Divine Order and its resultant cause and effect. I was a devoted student of John Locke; one of the more prominent English metaphysicians who would later shape the life and spiritually advanced wisdom of Ralph Waldo Emerson. I believed slavery was a miscarriage of justice that would inflict retribution on many generations to come. Although I did own slaves I considered them to be my extended family for reasons I will discuss later. I never sold and thereby separated loved ones from each other. I knew this was the true meaning of "What God hath joined together let no man put asunder." It was a common practice among slave owners to break up families who were joined together by the bonds of love for

Sally Hemings.
Portrait by Barbara Kiwak.

financial gain. This was something I never allowed. If a slave were born at Monticello they stayed the rest of their natural life unless they decided they wanted to leave or if the general slave population wanted them to leave. At times some did want to be with others they loved who lived elsewhere. Every effort was made to facilitate such desires. It was a cruel world away from Monticello as slaves were routinely seized, captured and sold by opportunists who sought to gain from this inhuman and ungodly scourge upon humanity.

I always understood slavery was doomed to extinction and I was able to lay the groundwork for its eventual demise by means of the Constitution which I was given the responsibility of creating. For the first time in the history of humanity, freedom of speech, freedom to worship as one pleased and personal freedom in general were guaranteed by our Constitution and became the law of the land. Can you imagine freedom guaranteed by law, although a blind eye was turned when it came to slavery as well as equality for women, both of which would eventually have to be reckoned with? Up to this point personal freedom was something that was spoken of by prophets and philosophers but was

Thomas Jefferson's Secret Life

never written into the law of the land for the protection of its citizens. I knew at the time I authored this generic phrase in the constitution, it would take many generations before "all men were created equal" would be interpreted as "all men, women and children of all race, color and creed." Yet, I had set in motion something revolutionary in the history of mankind and in doing so I became quite a controversial figure.

I accomplished much in my lifetime and the catalog of my achievements is stunning in breadth and depth. I was a lawyer, architect, violinist, inventor, a state legislator, a Governor, an Ambassador, a Secretary of State, a university president, a Vice President and the third President of the United States. As you already know, I was the principal architect of Declaration of Independence which was my crowning achievement. I wanted to end slavery but gave up the fight in order to be elected President. I was responsible for the Louisiana Purchase which doubled the size of the United States. After retiring from public service in in 1810 I devoted much of my time to establishing the University of Virginia. President Kennedy would later pay homage to me when he described an event honoring a group of Nobel Laureates as "the most extraordinary collection of human knowledge gathered together at the White House since Thomas Jefferson dined here alone." I was considered a polymath who also spoke five languages. In spite of all my wisdom, knowledge, experience and influential friends, when I passed on I was $100,000 in debt.

Although Sally was in her teens when we began our thirty eight year relationship, I eventually grew to love her very deeply even though I was thirty years older than her. At the time I was living in France serving as the American Ambassador. The year was 1787 she made the voyage to help care for my young children by my wife Martha who had passed away in 1782. I arranged for Sally to be trained in all the fashions of the day, dressmaking, sewing, hair design and all niceties that France had to offer so that she might become an able governess to a proper young lady. In the process she became a proper young lady herself. Her brother James was already with me in France having come there to learn the art of creating French cuisine. I soon found myself in the uncompromising position of becoming attached to beautiful young women whom our society back home in Virginia considered to be a lowly slave girl. It should be understood as long as Sally and James were living on French soil they were free according to French law but they both chose to return to Monticello with me and resume their lives as so called "slaves." This alone should attest to the fact that our lives were harmonious and intertwined with familial feelings. It was considered to be quite a privilege to live and work under the protection of such an honored statesmen as myself. I wanted to be able to declare my love for Sally and to experience the world with her but as a future President of the United States who would hold many different positions in government throughout the years to come; it was absolutely out of the question. There was an unwritten law at that period in time which said it was permissible to have a slave mistress but it was not acceptable to acknowledge any sort of relationship or feelings of love which may have existed. I was therefore entangled in the hypocrisy of a doomed culture. I had to suffer its interminable punishment in order to fulfill my obligations to my country, one of which was to see that this sort of prejudice would come to an eventual end.

I was sure I could be a continual force for change by accepting higher office and it was my destiny to do so. All through my many years in Washington my heart ached for my two families back in Virginia, one of which I could acknowledge and one I could not. The fact that Sally was three quarters white meant our children were seven eights white, but the law was clear in as far as anyone who had a trace of African blood was considered a slave to be denied freedom regardless of the fairness of their skin.

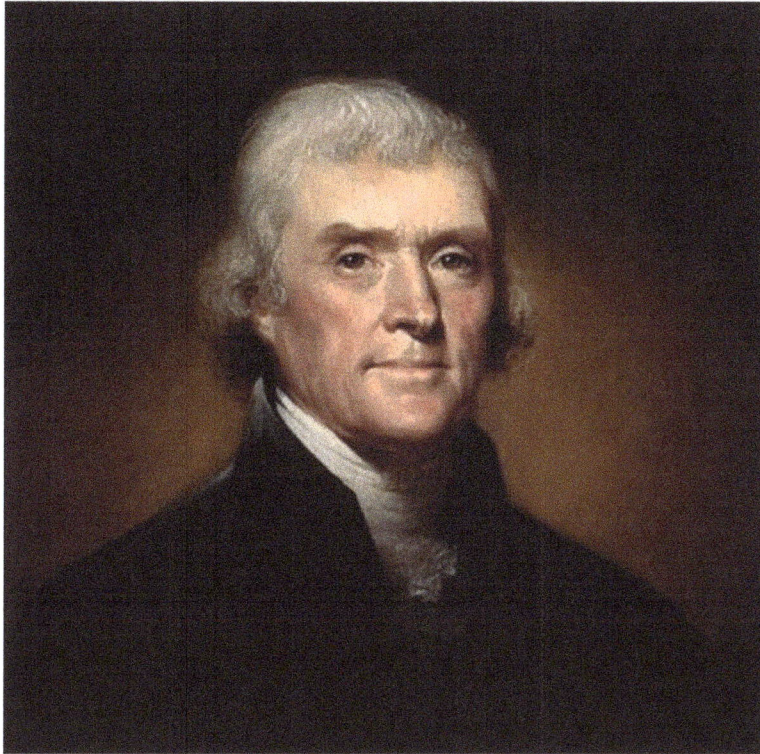

Thomas Jefferson.

Sally herself could have easily passed for white. Nonetheless, the task of being a Washington hostess on my behalf fell to my daughter Patsy, my daughter by my wife Martha. I would have loved to have Sally with me in Washington during my many years of service but it was simply not possible due to the prejudice that was engrained in our society at that period in time. When I retired from public service in 1810, I was able to enjoy my remaining years with Sally and our mutual and respective families.

The truth was, interracial marriage could never be a consideration and furthermore it was actually illegal in the state of Virginia where I lived. Even if it weren't illegal I believe if I ever dared to marry Sally I might have been executed by the diehard proponents of slavery who were quite a force to be reckoned with at the time. Hangings were frequent and sanctioned by the churches with regard to slaves who were considered to be without souls. They were relentlessly terrorized in order to keep them in submission. The primary motivation behind slavery was always to make a profit. Slaves were bought, sold and traded like cattle. They were routinely separated from loved ones on the premise that unhappy slaves worked harder than peaceful and contented slaves. I knew this was a horrible injustice against humanity. I also knew full well I was protecting my slaves from the predatory society that existed at the time. There was a harmony that existed at Monticello and my charges were quite content

Thomas Jefferson's Secret Life

to live under the protection of such an influential person such as myself, one of high social position, integrity and morality. All were treated with kindness, understanding and compassion. Monticello was actually a "Safe House" where we were able to live in peace and dignity. All were happy to do their share but Monticello was never a profitable proposition being as humane treatment was not a viable means of competing in the free markets with other plantation owners who had the distasteful competitive advantage of extracting every last "drop of blood" from their slaves. In addition, we provided for our elderly which was always a costly affair. They were able to enjoy their remaining years with family members rather than being sold off to the highest bidder when they were no longer able to do a full day's work. Eventually most all of our slave population was related to Sally or me in one way or another. They were either our children, grandchildren, or her siblings, either of which eventually had grown to maturity and had families of their own. So I suppose you might say we were one big happy family although truthfully current day historians do not realize it was this type of situation. It was something everyone knew and accepted at that time yet somehow the relevance of our interrelatedness was forgotten in the context of history. The same was true of the interrelated population of many of the other plantations, although many owners did not feel a kinship to their darker progenies simply because of the color of their skin. I could not allow myself to feel this way and more especially in light of my relationship with Sally. Visiting foreign dignitaries who did not understand our way of life were taken by surprise to see one or more of the servants who looked very much like me, but to those who understood our culture, it was quite a normal occurrence.

My being a Statesmen who held one high office or another over many years, required me to be frequently entertaining, which in turn required a large staff and incurred great expense for which I was rarely adequately reimbursed. There was a dignity and elegance which was possessed by all who lived at Monticello and I believe it had a great deal to do with my personal influence, one of courtesy and refinement coupled with kindness and Southern hospitality. I was often quoted as saying "All who lived on the mountain were my family" and I sincerely meant it more than anyone who was looking back in history could have readily realized. Everyone had a specific task to perform and was an integral part of a team effort which made Monticello a wonderful place to live and it was so, beyond one's imagination. All were honored and respected for their individual contribution. It was only I who had the worry of financial matters and truthfully, it was a heavy cross to bear. Everyone else at Monticello was free of such burdens and the result was spiritual and racial harmony that most people will never experience in their lifetime. We all loved and respected each other. It was always my greatest desire to retire which I was eventually able to do in 1810. Up until then my life was a constant struggle to constantly try to adapt from the peace and tranquility of Monticello to the treachery, responsibility and inharmonious existence associated with governmental office.

After my demise at the age of eighty three, Monticello was designated a national monument in my honor. The year was 1826. By 1831 congress refused the necessary funding to maintain Monticello as anti-slavery sentiment was beginning to mount. At this point Monticello reverted to private ownership. The fact that I had owned slaves had branded me a hypocrite. It seems history has vindicated me to some degree as Monticello has once again become a national monument although to this day it is still privately funded. I can only say in my defense I have always believed "All men, women and children are created equal in God's eyes" and I offer as proof my profound contribution to humanity namely "The Declaration of Independence." This groundbreaking, extraordinary and historic document has been a model for freedom loving people throughout the world since its creation. Could I have been oblivious to its intent and eventual consequences? Freedom and equality for all of God's children was always my primary mission in life although it may not have seemed that way to those who do not understand the difficulty of living among the radical injustices of our times and the intolerable behavior that was so ingrained in our society.

To be a slave with valid identification papers stating who owned that particular slave was somewhat like having a passport in a foreign country. It established the slave's legal right to walk the streets without being set upon. It was considered a high crime to steal a slave from another slave holder. Slaves were also considered real property and one had to relinquish ownership if he were deeply in debt and his creditors were demanding payment. My eventual demise was a devastating blow to our slave population. Sally was one of five slaves I was able to free, including our sons Madison and Eston Hemmings. Two of our older children Beverly (a male) and Harriet had left Monticello a few years earlier. Being as my slaves were considered part of my assets I was unable to free them all and the remainder were sold off to satisfy my debts. This was a heartbreaking affair. I was devastated by the thought of these poor souls being sold and possibly being separated from their loved ones. I also worried a great deal how those who were freed would survive and adapt in such treacherous environment. They were not prepared for the cruel ways of the world which existed away from Monticello. Unfortunately at the time of my death I was deeply in debt and was unable to provide Sally and our children with an adequate amount of money to make an acceptable and safe life for them. Patsy, my sole surviving child by my wife Martha was left penniless as well. She also lived at Monticello with her eleven surviving children. Our wonderful way of life had come to a disastrous end. We had had an extended family within which all were valued for their unique contribution. I had hoped one day our country could experience the same moral and racial harmony. It was a paradise of peace, harmony, love and spiritual contentment and could be compared to a medieval fortress that protected its fortunate inhabitants from the continual onslaughts of the brutally unconscious society within which we all were forced to live.

Was I a slave to my responsibilities? I had a constant financial struggle to deal with plus the obligatory involvement in trying to keep our fledgling country on its intended course. After my retirement things were worse yet as there was little or no income available from my government service. This was a terrible emotional burden on me while all who lived at Monticello were free of any such problems. They lived a carefree and happy life and I did everything in my power to make it so. The fact that everyone was free from financial obligations and was protected from the unsavory and cruel world that existed away from Monticello was a tremendous freedom that very few people ever have the privilege of enjoying in their lifetime regardless of the time period they lived in. It was true freedom within which spirituality was able to blossom. It was a great experiment and it proved to me that God-centered people of all race, creed or color could live in harmony if they so desired.

Unfortunately, I was one of those who craved material possessions and was willing to sell myself into voluntary slavery in order to acquire and maintain them. Coupled with all my unavoidable responsibilities this materially minded mentality only added to my difficulties in life. If I could find any fault with myself it would be for the fact that I never realized this until it was too late to recover from the damage done to my peace of mind and tranquility. Surely, my possessions possessed me and thereby hindered me from adequately providing for my loved ones. The fact was my lifestyle always exceeded my income and this was an ongoing burden to bear. Of course it didn't help matters that I had an extremely large number of dependents who I never turned my by back on no matter how difficult things became.

Thomas Jefferson's Secret Life

The greatest enduring happiness in my life was the fact that I was blessed with the love of a wonderful women whom society judged to be inferior but, in reality, was extremely capable of being my guiding light in anything I attempted, including but not limited to the affairs of state in which I participated for the greater part of my long life. I had mentored her over the years and there came a point where she slowly and assuredly became my advisor and confidant. She was endowed with the wisdom born of societal oppression and unfulfilled desires. She longed to be by my side wherever and whenever I answered the call to duty yet this was this an impossibility that weighed heavily on us both. We had created a paradise within the midst of a world rampant with ignorance and prejudice. Our world was modeled after "The Declaration of Independence" which I had created, whereby all men, women and children were understood to be created equal. Yet to all outward appearances our little society seemed devoid of all the qualities I have described. The answer was quite a simple one. In order to understand the wonder of life at Monticello, one had to be spiritually advanced to the degree that would be capable of participating in this Shangri-La like environment. To the unsuspecting outsiders it seemed like an average plantation and what was not outwardly apparent was the spiritually based peace of mind and the resultant blissful life that emanated from the brotherly love and emotional freedom possessed by all who lived at Monticello. We had created a successful microcosm of the new world that I envisioned would eventually evolve from our young country's noble experiment, based on the expanded premise I would have loved to have been able to include in The Declaration of Independence, that "All men, women and children of all race, color or creed are created equal and therefore equally endowed by God with certain inalienable rights among them being life, liberty and the pursuit of happiness."

In retrospect and looking back into history from a vantage point of over two hundred years, what I have related to you may seem a bit barbarian and I am sure in many respects it was, but it must not be overlooked that we had what amounts to a large extended family, that provided much love to all involved. We actually could not have survived without mutual caring, cooperation and respect, something that seems to be painfully absent in your modern day society. It was a team effort to run Monticello which was, in effect, was the family business. It was our sole means of survival. We had no government assistance of any kind, nor would we have taken it if it were available. It was a different time, a different world and a different way of life. After my political life came to an end we knew very little of the outside world and what we did know took weeks and months to learn and maybe that was the biggest blessing of all. Our world was a world within a world and it seemed the less contact we had with the outside world the happier we were able to be.

by Paul Martin

A note from Sally Hemings,

Mr. Jefferson and I have known...had lived under the same roof...the same residence since I was three years of age. Ms. Martha is...was my sister...half-sister. We have the same father, but that doesn't matter, not here. Mr. Jefferson is a wonderful man, very passionate, worldly, and very intelligent. He's written books, laws, and can convince people black is white if he wants to do so...fiercely passionate.

But he has this softness about him, a fear within him that he hides from all the world...but me. You would have to be with him when he's all alone. When no one is here to ask "world questions." At the right moment when the quiet is so still...if the breeze were to blow it would be as if a lion roared... in that moment, you look into his eyes and they glisten...color is gone...deep pools of fears and loss and...aloneness. It would break your heart. A lesser man would die from the pain...not Mr. Jefferson. He calls to me. I bring back the color to his eyes, the strength to his body and mind...give a safe place for his soul to be. He knows I will be here. I cannot leave him...even if I could, I would stay. He gave me that chance in Paris...to stay free...I came back. My children will live free. He gave his word. He is a man of his word...his beautiful flowing words. What does it matter, what happens in the outside world. It does not come inside our Monticello.... Here there is beauty, education, culture...all that will prepare my children for their own lives...outside...in the free world. This is my world...our world...our Eden. Here it is safe for Mr. Jefferson and me...it does not matter what is said out there...we are here... untouchable in this beautiful place. I see in his eyes the world as it should be...I live in those eyes...a secret moment in all time...our time.

by Ms. T. Valada-Viars

Videos

Christ's Life in Art and Music

Visit Youtube Link
https://youtu.be/1xQqjhXM4J4

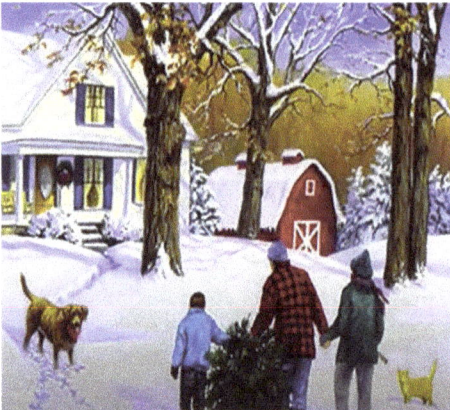

I'm Going Home for Christmas

Visit Youtube Link
https://youtu.be/mNhVLEVpLPE

The Freedom of the USA

Visit Youtube Link
https://youtu.be/3c5zxTKZEuY

Your notes

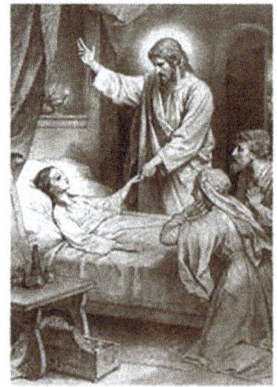

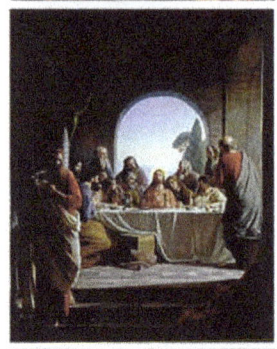

www.ingramcontent.com/pod-product-compliance
Lightning Source LLC
Chambersburg PA
CBHW040259100426
42811CB00011B/1316